MINI·ATLAS·OF
BRITAIN

Bartholomew
Duncan Street, Edinburgh EH9 1TA

Printed by Bartholomew in Edinburgh, Scotland

Published by Bartholomew
Duncan Street
Edinburgh
EH9 1TA

1st Edition 1987
Revised Edition 1990

ISBN 0 7028 0789 3

C/B3461

CONTENTS

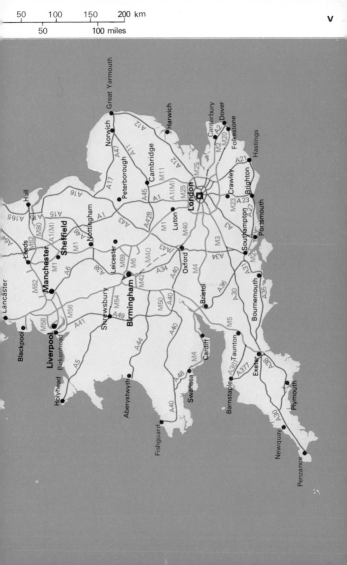

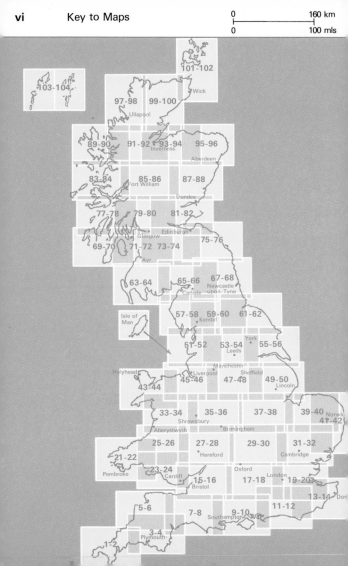

Page 103-104 **KEY** Page 1-102

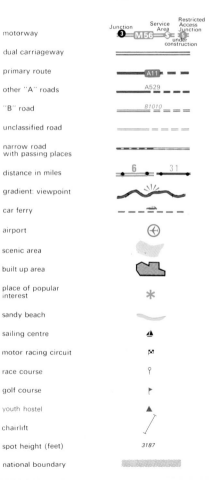

	motorway
	dual carriageway
	primary route
	other "A" roads
	"B" road
	unclassified road
	narrow road with passing places
	distance in miles
	gradient: viewpoint
	car ferry
	airport
	scenic area
	built up area
	place of popular interest
	sandy beach
	sailing centre
	motor racing circuit
	race course
	golf course
	youth hostel
	chairlift
	spot height (feet)
	national boundary

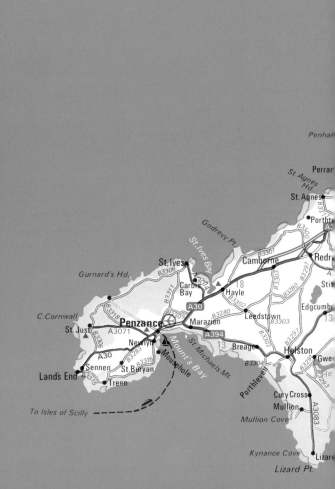

1

Penha

Perran

St. Agnes
Hd.

St. Agnes

Portht

B3300

A

Godrevy Pt.

Camborne

Redr

A

St. Ives

B3301

Sti

Gurnard's Hd.

B3306

18

Carbis
Bay

Hayle

B3280

B3297

B3303

Edgcumb

13

C.Cornwall

St. Just

B3318

Penzance

Marazion

Leedstown

B3303

B3302

A30

A3071

A30

Newlyn

A394

13

Breage

Helston

Gwe

B3283

St. Michaels Mt.

Porthleven

B3304

B329

Sennen

St.Buryan

B3315

Mouschole

Mount's Bay

B3293

He

Land's End

B3315

Treen

Cury Cross

Mullion

A3083

To Isles of Scilly

Mullion Cove

Kynance Cove

Lizar

Lizard Pt.

8km
5miles

Pentire Hd.
Padstow Bay
Port Isaac
Polzeath
St. Kew Highway
Fivelanes
A30
S. Petherwin
Hd.
Padstow
Rock
Bolventor 276
B3267
B3314
B3254
Pentire
t.
han
eps
Little Petherick
Wadebridge
B3274
A39
B3284
Camel
Bodmin
Moor
892
Upton Cross
B3254
Kellyb
B3274
A389
703
St. Ive
Bodmin
13
Fowey
Dobwalls
Liskeard
Lanivet
A389
A38
A390
W. Taphouse
St. Columb Major
St. Columb Minor
A30
Victoria
12
Lostwithiel
B3254
B3292
St. Gerr
A3058
Indian Queens
A389
Pelynt
B3359
A387
Fraddon
B3274
St. Blazey
B3269
20
Polba
A3271
24
A3058
B3279
W. Looe E. Looe
B3253
A39
St. Austell
A3082
Fowey
St. George's I.
A387
30
A390
B3273
Gribbin Hd.
Polperro
Wh
14
Grampound
Fowey
St. Austell Bay
Probus
Truro
B3287
Tregony
Mevagissey
Fal
Dodman Pt.
B3078
Philleigh
Portloe
A3076
Gerrans Bay
Nare Hd.
St. Mawes
Zone Pt.
Carrick Roads
uth Bay
verne
k
d.

8km
5miles

Bickleigh

Cadbury

estone

Bow

Crediton

Tedburn
St.Mary

ckernwell

Pocombe Br.

EXETER

Broad
Clyst

Whimple

Talaton

Honiton A35

B3185

B3181

B3176

A373

A30

A396

B3185

A377

B3212

B3177

B3174

Ottery
St.Mary

Colyford

B3176

Clyst Honiton

Clyst St.Mary

Newton
Poppleford

Topsham

A3052

B3174

Beer

Sidford

A376

Sidmouth

Exminster
Kennford

Moretonhampstead

Teign

AL PARK

Haytor
Vale

Bovey
Tracey

Chudleigh

Woodbury

B3179

A376

Budleigh Salterton

Starcross

Eye

A316

A319

Exmouth

B3212

B3214

Ilsington

A38

Drumbridge

Dawlish

B3192

B3381

Kingsteignton

B3195

Teignmouth

Bickington

A383

A381

**Newton
Abbot**

A380

B3199

*Babbacombe
Bay*

urton

A381

igh

46

A384

A380

A3022

Hopes Nose

Torquay

A385

A385

Totnes

Paignton

B3210

Dart

Brixham

Berry Hd.

Halwell

B3207

Churston Ferrers

B3205

Dartmouth

Kingswear

A379

Stoke Fleming

Kingsbridge

Stokenham

Slapton

one

38

Torcross

Hallsands

be

**East
Portlemouth**

Start Pt.

Prawle Pt.

d.

To Channel Islands

Otter

A30

A35

B3161

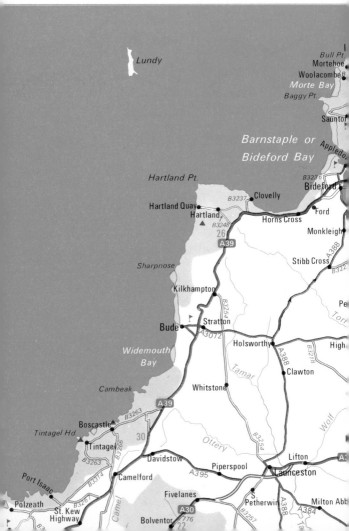

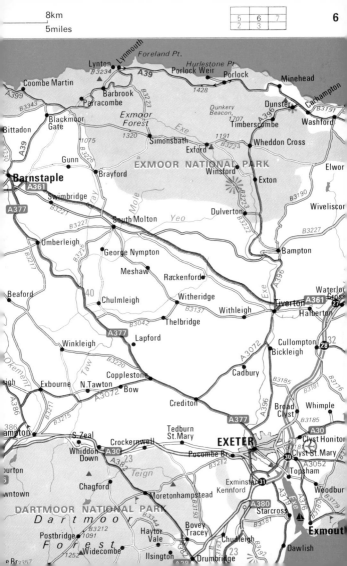

8km
5miles

| 5 | 6 | 7 |
| 2 | 3 | |

Lynmouth
Foreland Pt.
Lynton
B3234
A39
Hurlstone Pt.
Porlock Weir
Porlock
Minehead
Coombe Martin
A399
Barbrook
Parracombe
B3223
1428
Dunster
Carhampton
B3191
Blackmoor Gate
Exmoor Forest
Dunkery Beacon
1707
Timberscombe
Washford
B3343
1075
1320
Simonsbath
Exe
1191
Wheddon Cross
Bittadon
A39
B230
Gunn
Brayford
Exford
B3224
Elwor
Barnstaple
EXMOOR NATIONAL PARK
Winsford
Exton
A361
Swimbridge
Taw
Mole
Dulverton
Wiveliscor
A377
B3221
B3227
South Molton
Yeo
B3223
B3227
Umberleigh
B3226
B3227
George Nympton
Bampton
B3222
B3190
Beaford
40
Meshaw
Rackenford
Witheridge
B3137
Waterlo
Cross
Chulmleigh
B3042
Thelbridge
Withleigh
Tiverton
A361
Halberton
32
Winkleigh
A377
Lapford
Exe
Cullompton
28
B3220
Bickleigh
Okement
Copplestone
Taw
Cadbury
B3181
B3716
Exbourne
N.Tawton
Bow
A3072
Broad
Clyst
B3185
Whimple
A386
B3211
B3215
Crediton
A377
A396
Whipton
A30
Clyst Honiton
ampton
386
S.Zeal
Crockernwell
Tedburn St.Mary
EXETER
Clyst St.Mary
ourton
Whiddon Down
A30
23
A382
Pocombe Br.
B3212
30
Topsham
wntown
Chagford
Moretonhampstead
B3193
Exminster
Kennford
31
A3
Woodbur
B3176
B3179
DARTMOOR NATIONAL PARK
Teign
A380
Starcross
Exmout
Dartmoor
Postbridge
1091
Haytor Vale
Bovey Tracey
Chudleigh
B3381
Dawlish
B3357
1252
Forest
Widecombe
Ilsington
Drumbridge
A38
B3192

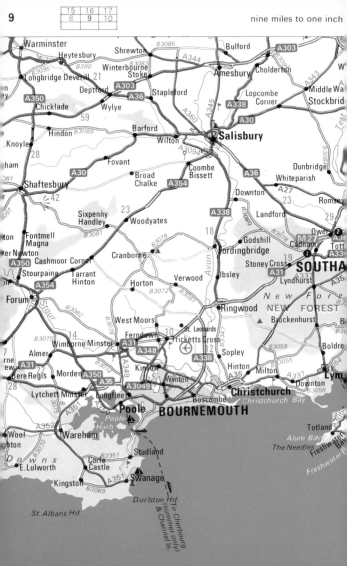

Warminster
Heytesbury
Shrewton
B3086
Bulford
A303
B390
Winterbourne
Stoke
Amesbury
Cholderton
A343
Longbridge Deverill 21
Deptford
A303
A36
Stapleford
Lopcombe
Corner
Middle Wa
Stockbrid
Chicklade
Wylye
A338
A30
59
Barford
Hindon *B3089*
Wilton
A360
A345
Salisbury
Knoyle
28
Fovant
Coombe
Bissett
Dunbridge
Shaftesbury
A30
Broad
Chalke
A354
Downton
A36
Whiteparish
Romsey
42
23
A338
Landford
29
Sixpenny
Handley
Woodyates
18
Godshill
Fordingbridge
19
Ower
Cadnam
Tott
Fontmell
Magna
B3081
B3078
Cranborne
Stoney Cross
SOUTHA
Newton
A350 Cashmoor Corner
Verwood
Ibsley
A31
Lyndhurst
Stourpaine
Tarrant
Hinton
Horton
B3072
B3081
Ringwood
New Fore
NEW FOREST
Brockenhurst
Forum
A354
B3092
West Moors
B3078
St. Leonards
B3347
B3055
Boldre
14
Ferndown
10
Tricketts Cross
B3058
B3075
Wimborne Minster
A31
A348
Sopley
Milton
Lym
Almer
A338
Hinton
A35
Downton
Bere Regis
Morden
A350
Kinson
Winton
A337
28
Lytchett Minster
A35
A3049
Winton
Christchurch
Longfleet
Boscombe
Christchurch Bay
Wool
A352
Poole
BOURNEMOUTH
ghton
Wareham
Poole
Harb
Totland
Alum Bay
The Needles
Freshwater
Downs
Studland
B3351
E. Lulworth
Corfe
Castle
Swanage
Freshwater B
Kingston
B3069
A351
Durlston Hd.
St. Albans Hd.
To Cherbourg
(summer only)
& Channel Is.

To Vlissingen

Westgate on Sea

Margate

Kingsgate

North Foreland

Birchington

Reculver

Herne Bay

stable

B2205

A299

I. of Thanet

Herne

Upstreet

Sarre

Minster

A253

Broadstairs

B2048

2052

Ramsgate

A255

Stour

Pegwell Bay

Bleam

A290

Sturry

Wingham

A28

Richborough

anterbury

A257

Ash

A257

Littlebourne

Sandwich

A258

A28

B2046

Aylesham

Eastry

Deal

Walmer

B2057

Denton

DOWNS

Elham

B2065

Selstad

A2

A256

St.Margarets at Cliffe

A260

Lyminge

Alkham

B2060

Temple Ewell

A258

South Foreland

To Zeebrugge

Sellindge

B2068

A20

Dover

To Oostende

Newingreen

B2067

Lympne

Folkestone

Sandgate

Dunkerque

To Calais

y Canal

d) A259

Hythe

Dymchurch

urch

St Mary's Bay

Littlestone-on-Sea

Greatstone-on-Sea

To Boulogne

To Boulogne

Dungeness

S T R A I T   O F   D O V E R

To Zeebrugge

To Oostende

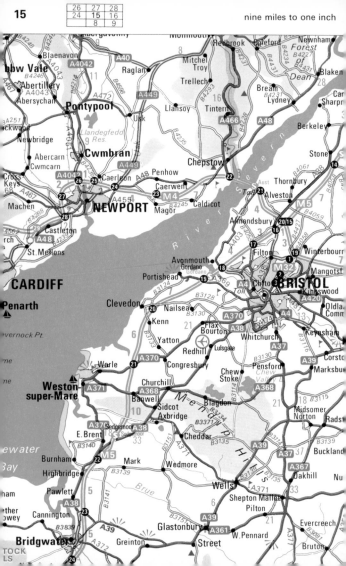

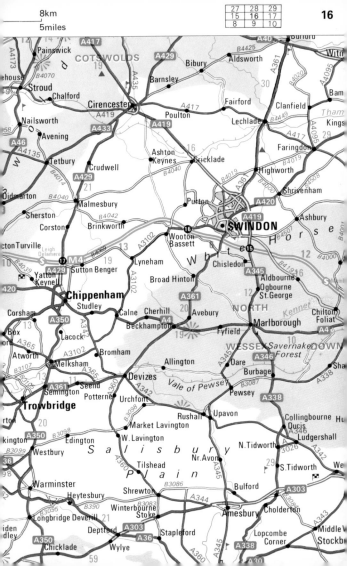

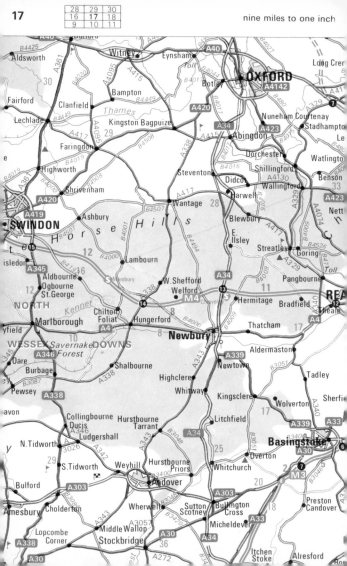

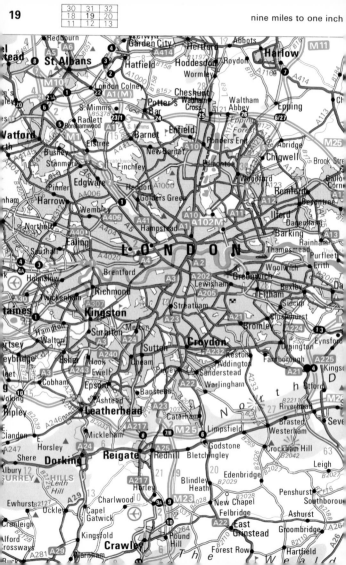

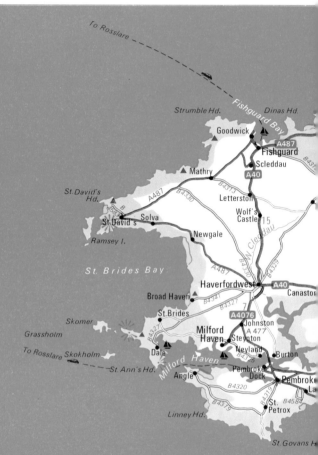

Ynys Lochtyn
Llangranog
Aberporth
Sarnau
Synod Inn
Ystrad Aeron
Temple Bar
Llangybi
B4342
Teifi
A4333
A4333
A487
B4333
Sea
Blaenporth
Cardigan
Llechryd
Bridell
Cribyn
Ffostrasol
Rhyd-Owen
Llanwnen
Lampeter
A475
A486
A482
C
B4571
Horeb
Llandyssul
Teifi
Llanybyther
Pumpsaint
Newcastle
Emlyn
A484
B4333
A475
B4335
A486
B4336
Boncath
vyswrw
4332
Crymmych
Taf
Gwyddgrug
Llansawel
Talley
B4459
B4299
B4310
B4337
B4327
B4302
Trelech
dissilio
Llanboidy
Cynwyl Elfed
B4333
B4301
Llanegwad
A40
Llande
B4298
Carmarthen
15
A485
B4300
A483
Whitland
St.Clears
A40
A48
Llanarthney
Porth-y-Rhydd
Llandybi
Br
B4312
A48
B4459
B455
Llanddowror
ernspite
B4310
Taf
Tywi
Llanddarog
A4066
Llandyfaelog
B4306
Cross
Hands
Amm
A4297
Red Roses
Laugharne
B4309
Tumble
A483
Pendine
A4066
A4314
Ferryside
Pontyates
27
B4317
A48
Pont Abraham
Kidwelly
Llanon
Abraham
ty
undersfoot
Llanstephan
B4308
B4310
B4307
Hendy
48
Pontardulai
nby
Carmarthen Bay
Pembrey
B4317
Llanelli
A48
M
Pontardulai
Caldy I.
Burry Port
A484
B4296
Llwchwr
47
Worms
Burry Inlet
A4070
SWANSEA
Llanmadoc
B4271
Upr.Killay
A4118
A4067
GOWER
Gower
Black Pill
Llangennith
Llanddewi
A4118
B4436
Bishopston
Mumbles
Worms Hd.
Oxwich
B4247
B4593
Rhosili
Port Eynon
Oxwich Bay
Swa
To Cork

Gwyuugrug
Llansawel
Talley
Llanwrda
Llandovery
B4299
B4433
B4310
A40
A4069
Cwm Wysg Res.
Cynwyl Elfed
A485
Llanegwad
A40
Llangadog
Black Mountain
12
Twyn-llanan
1618
A4061
Carmarthen
A48
Llanarthney
Llandeilo
A483
A4298
B4300
B4297
Llandybie
Pen-y-
Porth-y-Rhydd
B4310
A476
B4310
Llandarog
B4306
Llandyfaelog
Tumble
Cross Hands
B4297
Bryn-amman
A474
A4068
Llanon
B4317
B4300
Ammanford
A483
A48
Pont Abraham
Ystalyfera
Ystra
B4308
Pontyates
A4138
Abram
Ferryside
A484
B4377
Kidwelly
B4308
Hendy
Pontardulais
Pontardawe
A474
Cryna
A4240
A465
Pembrey
B4377
A48
A4109
Llanstepha
B4312
Tawe
Burry Port
Llanelli
B4296
A483
M4
A465
Bay
Burry Inlet
Llwchwr
A4070
Morriston
Skewen
Neath
A4230
A4067
Briton Ferry
A4287
Llanmadoc
GOWER
Upr. Killay A4118
SWANSEA
A483
Mae
Llangennith
Gower
B4271
B4436
Black Pill
Aberavon
Port Talbot
A4118
Bishopston
Mumbles
M4
Llanddewi
Oxwich
B4247
Worms Hd.
Rhosili
Oxwich Bay
Port Eynon
Swansea Ba
Porthcawl
S
To Cork

B R I S T O L

Aberystwyth
Goginan
Ponterwyd
A44 *Rheidol*
Pentrebont
B4340 A4120
Devils Br.
B4574 *Ystwy*
A485
Llanilar B4575
Lledrod
Ysbyty Ystwyth
Llanrhystyd
Bronnant
Ystrad Meurig
Llansanffraid
B4337
Pontrhydfendigaid
A487
Cross Inn
Aberaeron
Aberarth
B4577 A485 A4343
Tregaron
New Quay
A482 B4576
B4342
A486 B4342
b
38
Ystrad Aeron
Synod Inn
Temple Bar
Llangybi
Teifi
m
Llyn Brianne Resr
B4338
Cribyn
A485
Llan
Sarnau
B4334
B4459
Llanwnen A475
Lampeter
a
Ffostrasol
A486
Rhyd-Owen
B4451 B4338
Horeb
Llandyssul
A482
C
A475 A486
B4335
Llanybyther
Cilycwm
A484 B4336
Pumpsaint
A483
Llandovery
B4299
Gwyddgrug
Llansawel
B4327 B4302
Cwm Wysg Res.
B4333
B4310
Talley
Llanwrda
A40069
12
Cynwyl Elfed
B4301
Llangadog
Twyn-llanan
Carmarthen
A485
Llanegwad
A40
Mountain
4298
A48
15
B4300 B4297 B4300
Llandeilo
A483
1618
Clears
A48
Llanarthney
Porth-y-Rhyd
A476
Black
Pen-y-
40
A40
B4312
Llanddarog
B4306
B4459
Llandybie
A4069
Llandyfaelog
Tumble
Cross Hands
Bryn-amman
A474 A4068
Ferryside
A484
B4317 B4309
Pontyates
27
A483
Ammanford
Ystalyfera
Llanstephan
Kidwelly
Llanon
Pont Abraham
Ystra
Crynar
Sawe

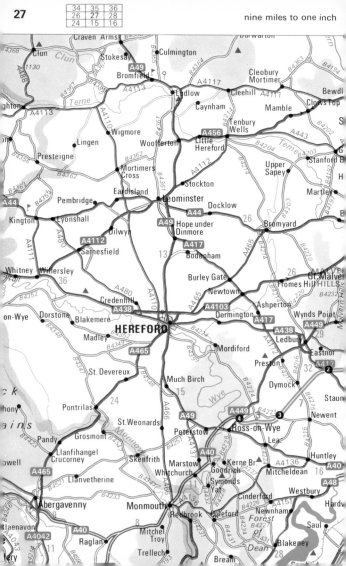

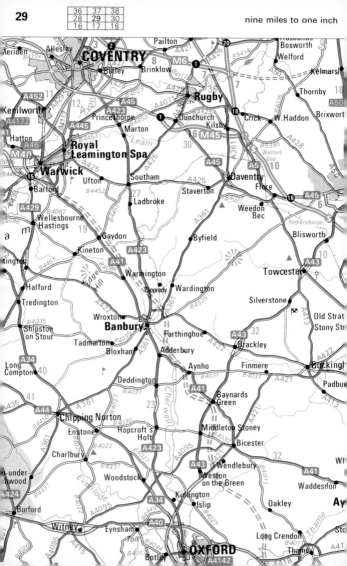

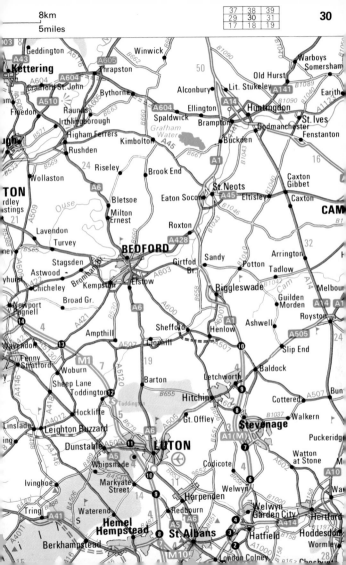

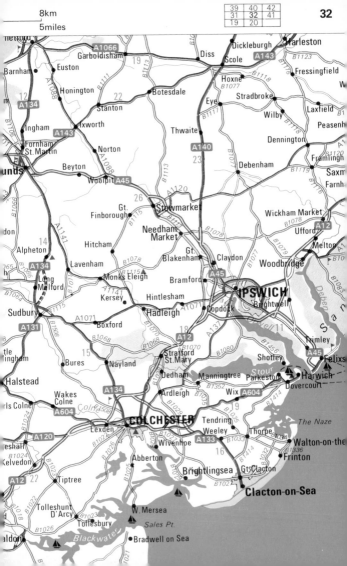

43	44	45
24	**33**	34
24	25	26

Beddgelert
A487
Dolbenmaen
A4085
Tremadog
B4411
Penrhyndeudraeth
Criccieth
Porthmadog

Blaenau
Ffestiniog
A470
B4407
Ffestiniog
A496
Maentwrog
B4410
Toll
B4573
Llyn
Trawsfynydd
Trawsfynydd

s
B4501
n
Llyn Celyn
B4931
A212
A4212
Bala
A494
B4391
B440
Bala L.
B4403

Harlech
Llanbedr
a d o g
y

32
A470
Llanuwchllyn
18
770
a

Tyn-y-groes
L.Vyrnwy
n

Llanaber
Barmouth
Arthog
A496
Llanelltyd
A470
Dolgellau
A493
Cross Foxes
1178
A470
Dinas Mawddwy
Mallwyd
957
Banw
t
u

Cader Idris
2927
938
Aberllefenni
16
Borris
A470
n
Llwyngwril
Llangelynin
B4405

Dyfi
A487
B4404
A489
Cemmaes Rd.
Llanbrynmair
Tywyn
Bryn-crug
Pennal
A493
Penegoes
Machynlleth
Talerddig
23
Carno
Pontdo
M

Aberdyfi
N
18
B4353
Borth
Talybont
Nant-y-moch
Res.
Plynlimon
Fawr
Clywedog
Res.
B4518
Ll
B4569

Bow Street
A487
A4159
Goginan
1350
22
Severn
n

Aberystwyth
A44
Ponterwyd
Wye
A470
Llangurig
Pentrebont
Rheidol
Devils Br.
9
952
B4340
A4120
B4343
B4574
Llanit
Llanilar
B4518
B4574
n
a

Llanrhystyd
Lledrod
Ysbyty Ystwyth
Ystwyth
61

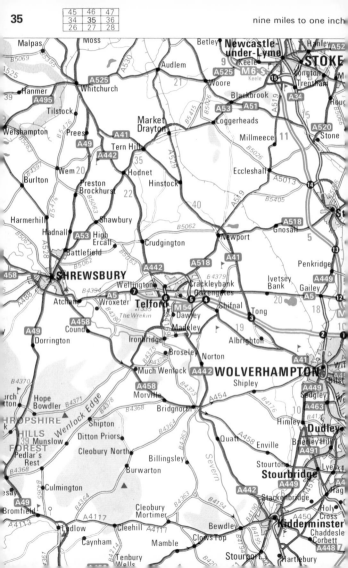

THE

WASH

NORFOLK

Benington
iston
A52

6
A52

Brancaster
Burn
Hunstanton
B1153

Heacham
Docking
B1155

B1454

Snettisham
Dersingham
B1155
B1454
43

Holbeach Marsh
Wolferton
Flitcham
B1153

Gedney Drove End
B1359

Castle Rising
Harpley
Great Massingham
B1440

4
A17
Holbeach
Sth Wootton
A148

Long Sutton
B1078
Gaywood
B1145

Sutton Br.
King's Lynn
A149
Gayton
B1153

A1101
A17
Terrington St. Clement
Li

rydd St. Mary
A47
Middleton
16

Sutton St. James
St. John's Highway
E. Winch
Newton

B1165
Setchey
A10
Narborough
Necto

dney Hill
B1169
11
Sth Runcton
Nar
Swaffham

Wisbech
Ouse
A134
A1122

21
Guyhirn
13
Outwell
Stradsett
A1065

B1411
B1169
Hilboro

605
A141
A1122
Nordelph
Downham Market
Stoke Ferry

March
Th
B1098
Hilgay
B1160

B1099
Southery
Methwold
A134
Mundford

B1093
New Bedford
18
Feltwell
B1386
32

Doddington
A10
A1101
Weeting
B1077
Thetfo

35
Littleport
Brandon

Chatteris
B1411
Lakenheath
Elveden

A142
Ely
A1065
Barnha

Sutton
B1104
Beck Row
12

rsham
Haddenham
Wilburton
Stretham
Isleham
Mildenhall
20
Icklingham
A13

Earith
A1123
13
Lark
B1112

Willingham
Soham
Fordham
A11
Barton Mills
Lackford

Cam
B1102

8km
5miles

Blakeney Cley Neybourne Sheringham
W. Runton Cromer
Overstrand
Letheringsett A149 A148 A140 B1159 Roughton Thorpe Market Mundesley
Binham Holt Paston
gham B1110
Edgefield Green Gunton
Saxthorpe A149 B1150 Happisburgh
Aylsham B1145 N. Walsham
Guist B1110 B1145 Cawston Bure Stalham Palling
N. Reepham A140 Marsham B1354 Coltishall The Catfield Waxhar
Elmham Bawdeswell Horstead Hoveton A1062 Martham Hors
E. Wensum Attlebridge Wroxham Broads A1064 Filby
Dereham Hockering Drayton Horsham Ranworth Walsham Bure
Honingham A1067 B1151 Thorpe Gorle
Yare Easton A47 NORWICH Blofield Acle
Kimberley Hethersett A11 Trowse Newton
Hingham Swardeston A146 Reedham A14
Wymondham B1113 Swainsthorpe Loddon
Ashwellthorpe A140 Haddiscoe
on B1077 Attleborough Long Hempnall B1332 Beccles A14
New Stratton B1135 Bungay Mettingham Nth. Co
Buckenham Pulham Homersfield A45 B112
E. Harling B1134 Brampton A12
Kenninghall B1077 Dickleburgh Harleston Halesworth Wang
66 Diss Scole A143 B1123 Reydon A1095
ham Hoxne Fressingfield Blythburgh
Botesdale Eye Stradbroke Walpole Bramfield B1387
nton B1117 Wilby Laxfield B1117 Westleto
Thwaite Peasenhall

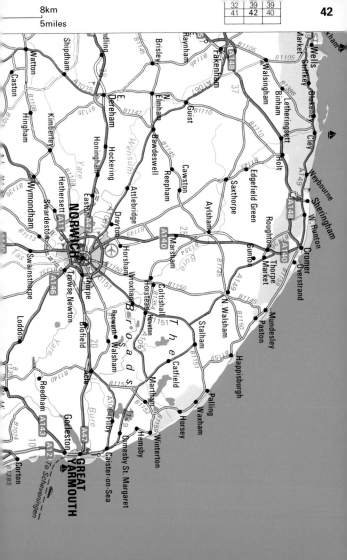

Carmel Hd.

Cemaes
Bay

Amlw

A5025

B5111

Llanfeathlu

A5025

*Alaw
Res*

Llanerchymedd

Llar

To Dublin & Dun Laoghaire

Holyhead Bay

Holyhead

Anglese

B5112

A5

Valley

B5109

Holy I.

B4245

Bryngwran

*Cefni
Res*

Gwalchmai

A51

Rhosneigr

A4080

Llanfaelog

21

B4422

A5

Aberffraw

Bethel

B4421

B4419

Newborough

Caernarfor

*Caernarfon
Bay*

A499

Clynnog-fawr

20

Llanaelhaearn

A48

Nefyn

B4417

A499

B4411

Lleyn Peninsula

B4354

B4417

A499

Llangwnnadl

B4415

Pwllheli

Sarn Meliteyn

B4413

Llanbedrog

Aberdaron

B4413

Abersoch

Treme

Bay

Porth
Neigwl

St. Tudwals Is.

Bardsey I.

Pencilan Hd.

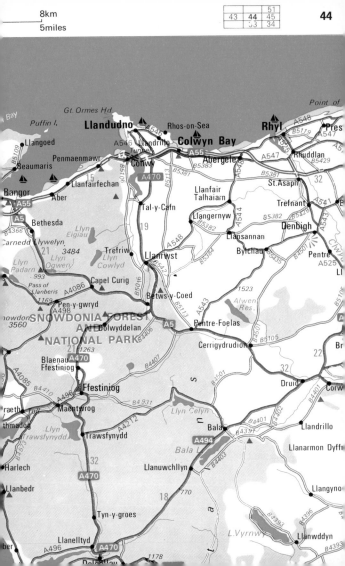

Point of

Bay

Puffin I.

Gt. Ormes Hd.

Llandudno

Rhos-on-Sea

Rhyl

Pres

A548

B5179

A547

Llangoed

Penmaenmawr

Llandrillo

Colwyn Bay

A546

A55

Rhuddlan

Conwy

Abergele

A547

B5429

Beaumaris

B5109

A55

B5113

B5381

A547

St.Asaph

32

Bangor

A5

Llanfairfechan

A470

B5381

Llanfair
Talhaiarn

Trefnant

A541

A55

Aber

15

Tal-y-Cafn

A544

Denbigh

Bethesda

B5106

Llangernyw

B5382

A543

A5

Llansannan

B5384

Llyn
Eigiau

Carnedd Llywelyn

21   *3484*

Trefriw

Bylchau

B5435

A501

Pentre

Llyn
Ogwen

Llyn
Cowlyd

Llanrwst

B5382

A525

Ll

Llyn
Padarn

.993

A5

B5016

19

A548

A543

1523

B5105

Pass of
Llanberis
1169

Capel Curig

A4086

Betws-y-Coed

*Alwen
Res.*

Pen-y-gwryd
A498

A5

A543

Pentre-Foelas

SNOWDONIA FOREST
snowdon
3560

AND

Dolwyddelan

A5

B5105

22

Br

NATIONAL PARK
21 *1263*

B4406

Cerrigydrudion

B5501

Blaenau
Ffestiniog

A470

A4085

B4407

32

A496

Druid

Corw

A4212

B4401

Ffestiniog

A4501

B4402

raeth
thmadog

B4391

Maentwrog

B4931

Llandrillo

Llyn
Trawsfynydd

B4573

Llyn Celyn

Bala

Llanarmon Dyffr

32

Trawsfynydd

n

A494

Bala L.

Harlec

A470

Llanuwchllyn

B4403

Llangyno

Llanbedr

18   *770*

a

L.Vyrnwy

Tyn-y-groes

B4393

B4396

Llanwddyn

A496

t

B4393

B4399

Llanelltyd

A470

1178

Dolgellau

Ainsdale

A565

Ormskir

Formby Pt.

Formby

B5195

B5195

Maghull

A59

Liverpool

Crosby

Aintree

Bay

Litherland

Bootle

New Brighton

Tunnel

Derby

Wallasey

Hoylake

A553

New Ferry

BIRKENHEAD

West Kirby

Mersey

Garston

Point of Air

Bebington

A540

Bromborough

M53

Eastham

Rhyl

A548

Prestatyn

Heswall

A5117

A41

B5118

Mostyn

Neston

A548

B5129

Capenhurst

A411

Abergele

A547

Rhuddlan

Greenfield

A5151

n Bay

A548

B5122

20

A547

Holywell

St. Asaph

Caerwys

A55

Flint

Whitby

nfair

A541

Halkyn

Conah's Quay

Shotton

A550

iaian

Trefnant

Bodfari

Northop

Queensferry

ngernyw

A544

B5382

B5429

Hawarden

A55

Denbigh

Mold

Buckley

Broughton

Llansannan

Pentre

A483

Bylchau

B5435

A525

Ruthin

Caergwrie

B5373

Rossett

1523

Llanbedr

A5104

B5105

A5430

Holt

Alwen

Res.

A494

Caergwrie

A534

tre-Foelas

A5

B5105

A525

A542

Wrexham

rrigydrudion

B5429

Bryneglwys

Marchwiai

Bar

A5104

A528

Dee

32

Ruabon

A483

Overton

Druid

Corwen

A5

A539

Llangollen

Bala

B4401

Glyn-Ceiriog

Chirk

B4500

Llandrillo

Ellesmere

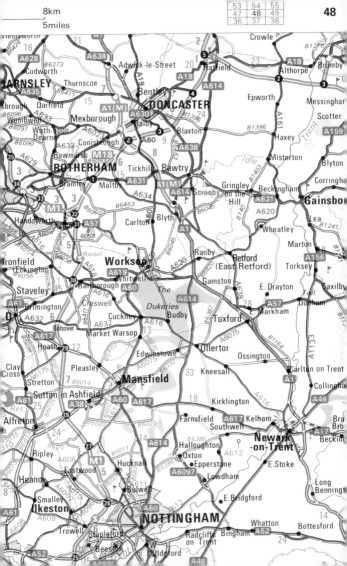

GRIMSBY
A1098
Cleethorpes
A18
Scartho
18
Humberston
ceby
Waltham
A16
B201
B1431
N.Thoresby
A1031
N. Somercotes
udborough
brook
Saltfleet
To Rotterdam
To Zeebrugge
A631
B1200
A1031
A157
Louth
Grimoldby
Legbourne
Mablethorpe
LINCOLNSHIRE
Withern
A157
A1104
A52
Sutton on Sea
A153
Burwell
A111
B1373
WOLDS▲
Scamblesby
Alford
A1104
B1449
Mumby
Chapel St. Leonards
A16
Ilceby Cross
A111
58
A1028
Willoughby
B196
Horncastle
A1115
Partney
Ingoldmells
A52
42
Winceby
Spilsby
Burgh le Marsh
A153
E.Keal
A158
B1183
B1195
Irby
Skegness
Revesby
A155
Stickford
A153
Wainfleet
Tumby
Gibraltar Pt.
Coningsby
Stickney
A52
New York
B1184
Old Leake
Wrangle
B1183
A16
Sibsey
A52
Benington
T H E
A1121
Boston
A52
B1192
Hunstanton
Branc
B1391
Kirton
Heacham
A17
Sutterton
B1454
W A S H

Millom
Ulverston
Askam
Cartmel
Grange over Sands
Arnside
Silverdale
BARROW-IN-FURNESS
Dalton
Bardsea
Gleaston
A590
A5087
Morecambe Bay
Walney I.
Rampside
Foulney I.
Morecambe
A5105
To Douglas
Hilpsford Pt.
Heysham
Lune
Galga
Cockerham
Fleetwood
Rossall Pt.
Pilling
A588
A587
Preesall
Garsta
Cleveleys
A585
St. Michaels on Wyre
A586
Poulton-le-Fylde
Singleton
BLACKPOOL
A584
A586
Fylde
M55
A585
4
23
3
Kirkham
A584
B261
B5259
A584
A5
Lytham St. Annes
Warton
Ribble
Longto
18

To Belfast & Stranraer
Pt. of Ayre
Bride
Ballaugh
Ramsey
A3
Kirk Michael
Sulby
16
Snaefell
2034
A565
Tarleton
Peel
A1
9
Grosby
Laxey
A2
A565
SOUTHPORT
B5244
A570
Rufford
A59
ISLE OF MAN
Onchan
Niarbyl B.
Douglas
To Heysham
B5243
Burscough Br.
Port Erin
3
Santan Hd.
Ainsdale
B5243
B567
Ormskir
Calf of Man
Port St. Mary
Castletown
To Liverpool
A565
B5195
A59
A577
A570
A5
To Dublin (Summer Only)
Formby
30
A59
B57
3
Maghull

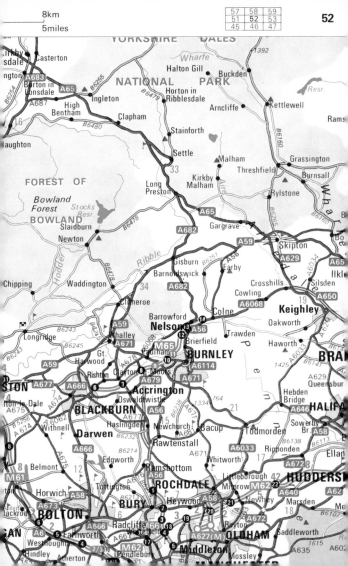

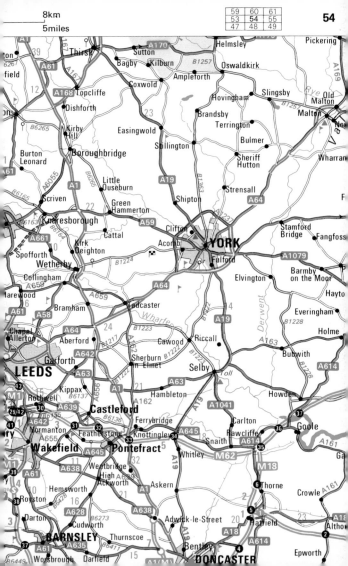

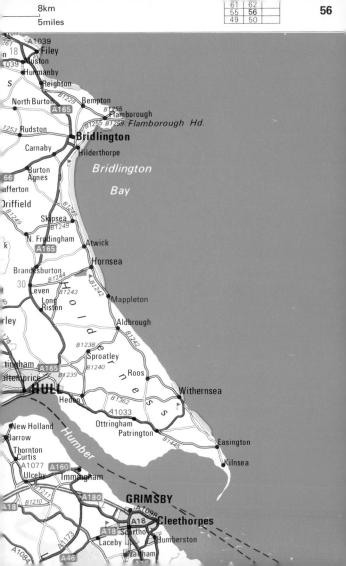

8km
5miles

A1039
Filey
Muston
Hunmanby
Reighton
North Burton   Bempton
A165   B1229
B1255
Flamborough
B1255 B1259   *Flamborough Hd.*
Rudston
Bridlington
Carnaby   Hilderthorpe
Bridlington
Burton
Agnes   *Bay*
66
fafferton
Driffield
B1249
Skipsea
B1249
N. Frodingham
A165   Atwick
Hornsea
Brandesburton
B1244
30   B1242
Leven   B1243
Long
Riston   Mappleton
rley
Aldbrough
H   B1242
B1238   o
Sproatley   l
B1240   d
tingham   A165   Roos   e
altemprice   B1239   r
HULL   n   Withernsea
Hedon   e
B1362   s
New Holland   41033   s
Barrow   Ottringham
Thornton   Patrington
Curtis   B1445
A1077   Easington
Ulceby   A160
Immingham   Kilnsea
Humber
B1210
GRIMSBY
A180   A1098
A18   **Cleethorpes**
A18
A18   Scartho   Humberston
A108   Laceby   Waltham
A46

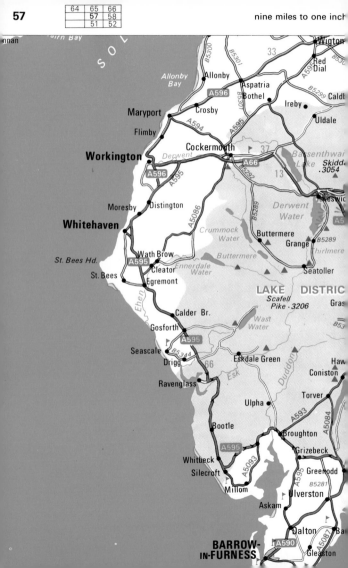

nnan

SO...

Cairn Bay

Wigton

B5300

33

Red
Dial

*Allonby
Bay*

Allonby

Aspatria

B5301

A596

Bothel

Ireby

Caldb

B5299

Crosby

Maryport

A594

A595

Uldale

Flimby

Workington

Cockermouth

Derwent

A66

37

Bassenthwai
Lake

13

A5292

Skidd
.3054

A596

A595

Keswic

A5

Moresby

Distington

A5086

*Derwent
Water*

B5289

Whitehaven

*Crummock
Water*

Buttermere

Grange

B5289

hirlmere

Wath Brow

A595

St. Bees Hd.

Cleator

*Ennerdale
Water*

Buttermere

Seatoller

St. Bees

Egremont

LAKE **DISTRIC**

*Scafell
Pike* .3206

Gras

Ehen

Calder Br.

*Wast
Water*

B5

Gosforth

A595

Seascale

B5344

Esk

Eskdale Green

Haw

Coniston

Drigg

66

Duddon

Torver

Ravenglass

Ulpha

A593

A5084

Bootle

Broughton

A595

Grizebeck

A595

Whitbeck

A5093

Greenodd

Silecroft

B5281

Millom

Ulverston

Askam

A590

**BARROW-
IN-FURNESS**

A590

A5087

Dalton

Gleaston

Ba

Armathwaite
High Hesket
21
Renwick
Kirkoswald
Lazonby
B6413
Gamblesby
Plumpton
B6412
Melmerby
A6
41
Langwathby
Penrith
40
Culgaith
3
B5288

Alston
Nenthead
2050 A689
Allenheads
Alston Moor
Wearhead
B6277
St. John's Chapel
Cross Fell · 2930
1962
Cow Green Resr.
Tees
Middleton in Teesdale

B5320
Pooley Bridge
A6
11
Bampton
Hawes Water
PARK
Shap.
M6
39
5

Appleby
A66
Warcop
Brough
A685
1436 A66 Bow
1578 B6276 Resr. Resr.
Balder
Ba

Crosby Ravensworth
Gt. Musgrave
Soulby
Kirkby Stephen
Nateby
Bowes Moor

Kentmere
1304
Tebay West
A6
38
Orton
B6261
28
Newbiggin
A685
Tebay

Staveley
A591
Grayrigg
8
B6257
Firbank
Lune
A683
B6259
B6270
Keld
Swale
Muker
Sw

Kendal
A685
37
A6
A684
B6255
Killington
Sedbergh
A684
981
Hawes
Askrigg
Bainbridge
Aysg

A65
8
B6254
Middleton
1421
Semmer W.

Crooklands
36
Lupton
21
Holme
Kirkby Lonsdale
Casterton
Burton in Kendal
A6
Whittington
A683
Burton in Lonsdale
A65
B6255
NATIONAL PARK
YORKSHIRE DALES
Wharfe
Halton Gill
Buckden
1392

6070
A687
High Bentham
Ingleton
Horton in Ribblesdale
B6479
Arncliffe
Hornby
16
Clapham
35A
35
forth
Pettell
Eden
Kentmere

Lanchester · Witton
Gilbert · Houghton-le-Spring · Hetton-le-Hole · Easington
A68 · Satley · B6296 · A691 · 14 · A167 · 6 · A690 · B1432
DURHAM · 3 · 5 · B1283 · Haswell · Peterlee
w Law · Wolsingham · B6299 · Brancepeth · A690 · B291 · A181 · Hart · A1086
Crook · Willington · 11 · Brandon · Coxhoe · Trimdon
tton-le-Wear · A689 · Spennymoor · B6291 · 6 · A177 · HARTLEPOOL
Wear · Weardale · A688 · Ferryhill
Bishop · A167 · Sedgefield · A19
Auckland · B6282 · Shildon · Wolviston · Greatham · A178
West · Newton · Aycliffe · A177 · A1086
Auckland · A688 · A6072 · A68 · 5 · A1(M) · MIDDLESBROUGH
Staindrop · B6279 · STOCKTON- · ON-TEES · Toll · South Bank
A688 · B6274 · B6275 · A68 · A167 · Thornaby-on-Tees · Eston · A171
6 Winston · Gainford · Sadberge · 11 · A66 · A19 · A174 · A173
Piercebridge · Stapleton · Long Newton · Nunthorpe · Gt. Ay
Caldwell · A66(M) · DARLINGTON · A67 · Yarm · A1044 · Stokesley
A66 · Aldbrough · Burworth · Croft · Crathorne · 28 · Broughton
Melsonby · Barton · Tees · Great Smeaton · Hutton Rudby · A172
Gilling · Scotch Corner · B1264 · A19 · Cleveland
Richmond · Catterick Bridge · B1263 · Wiske
A6108 · Catterick · A684
Downholme · A6136 · Rieval
A6108 · Clevela
eyburn · Patrick Brompton · Northallerton · B6125
Wensley · A684 · Ainderby Steeple · A19
Middleham · Leeming · S. Otterington · A170
Bedale · A168 · S. Kilvington · Sutton · B6
A6108 · Burneston · A1 · Bagby · Kilburn · B125
Masham · Well · Thirsk · Ampleforth
W. Tanfield · Kirklington · A61 · A61 · Coxwold · Bra
B6267 · B6268 · 39 · 12 · A168
Kirkby Malzeard · A168 · Topcliffe · Dishforth · 23
sgill · Ripon

Loftus
Staithes
Hinderwell
B1266
B1366
31
Danby
A171
Egton
Sleights
Lythe
Whitby
High Hawsker
Robin Hood's Bay
Goathland
930
Ravenscar
RK MOORS
AL PARK
A171
20
Rosedale
Abbey
Derwent
Lastingham
Cloughton
Burniston
Scalby
Scarborough
de
Middleton
A170
A165
Sinnington
Allerston
Seamer
Cayton
Pickering
44
Wykeham
A1039
Thornton
Dale
Brompton
B1261
Filey
B1415
Yedingham
A64
Folkton
18
Ganton
Staxton
Muston
B1258
A1039
Hunmanby
gsby
Rye Old
Sherburn
Reighton
Malton
W. Heslerton
Foxholes
North Burton
B125
Rillington
A165
Malton
A64
Wolds
Bempto
41
Norton

Runswick Bay
Pickering

Ailsa Craig

New Dailly
Old Dailly
Girvan

B741

B734

B741

Barr
C a r r
12
Polmad
Hill

51

A77

A714

Lendalfoot

Colmonell

Stinchar

Barrhill

Ballantrae

Tig

559

A71

B7027

Beneraird
1435

Cree

L. Dorn

G a

Bladnoch

To Larne

Corsewall Pt.

Glen App

Glen App

Kirkcolm

B738

B738

A718

B798

Cairnryan

Loch Ryan

A77

New Luce

Luce

Tarff

T h e   M o o r s

58

Leswalt

B738

The Rinns

Stranraer

Black

Cas.Kennedy

A75

Glenluce

A747

Machr
L

To Douglas (Summer Only)

A764

A77

A716

A751

A715

B7005

Portpatrick

B7042

Stoneykirk

Sandhead

of

Galloway

L u c e

Kirk of
Mochrum
Port William

B a y

Port Logan

A716

Drummore

B7065

B7041

Mull of Galloway

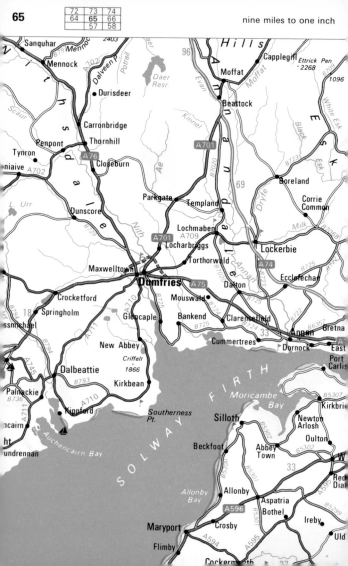

Sanquhar
Mennock
Mennoc
Dalveen P.
2403
96
Hills
Capplegill
Ettrick Pen
· 2268
B709
1096
Moffat
Daer Resr.
Beattock
Durisdeer
Carronbridge
Thornhill
Penpont
Tynron
niaive A702
A76
Closeburn
A701
B020
Kinnel
Boreland
Corrie
Common
Black Esk
White Esk
Esk
Scaur
Nithsdale
Scar
L. Urr
Dunscore
Parkgate
Templand
Lochmaben
A701 A709
Locharbriggs
Maxwelltown
Dumfries
Torthorwald
Lockerbie
Ecclefechan
A74
B725
Dalton
A75
Crocketford
Springholm
ssnmichael
18
Glencaple
New Abbey
Criffell
1866
Mouswald
Bankend
Clarencefield
Cummertrees
33
Annan
Gretna
Dornock
East
Port
Carlisl
Dalbeattie
Kirkbean
Palnackie
Kippford
ncairn
undrennan
Auchencairn Bay
Southerness
Pt.
Silloth
Beckfoot
Abbey
Town
Moricambe
Bay
Kirkbri
Newton
Arlosh
Oulton
W
SOLWAY FIRTH
Allonby
Bay
Allonby
Aspatria
Bothel
33
Red
Dial
Ireby
Uld
Maryport
Flimby
Crosby
Cockermouth
27

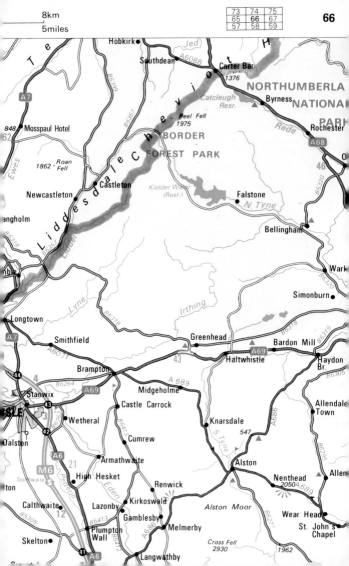

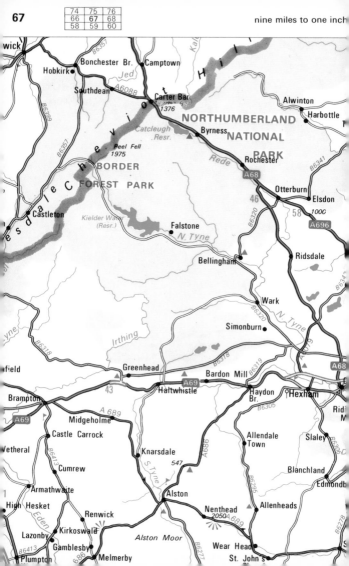

wick

Hobkirk

Bonchester Br.   Camptown

B6357

Jed

Southdean   *A6088*   Carter Bar
                          1376

Cheviot Hills

Alwinton

Harbottle

NORTHUMBERLAND

Catcleugh
Resr.   Byrness

NATIONAL

*Peel Fell
1975*

BORDER

PARK

Rochester

A68

B6341

FOREST PARK

Rede

Otterburn

Castleton

Kielder Water
(Resr.)

Falstone

N. Tyne

Elsdon
100C

A696

46

58

B6320

Bellingham

Ridsdale

B634

Wark

N. Tyne

Simonburn

Irthing

B6318

B6319

A68

field

Greenhead

Bardon Mill

Brampton

43

A69

Haltwhistle

B6318

Haydon
Br.

Hexham

Rid

A69

A 689

Midgeholme

Castle Carrock

Knarsdale

Allendale
Town

Slaley

B6305

B6320

Cumrew

547

A686

Blanchland

Edmondb

etheral

Armathwaite

B6413

S. Tyne

Alston

Nenthead
2050
A 689

Allenheads

B6295

B6278

High Hesket

Renwick

Eden

Lazonby   Kirkoswald

Alston Moor

Gamblesby

B6413

B6277

Wear Head

St. John's

Plumpton   Melmerby

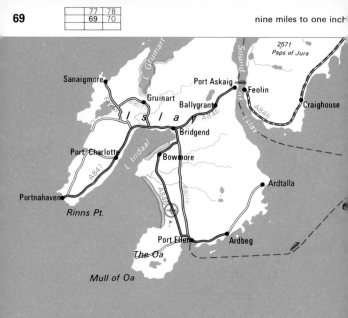

2571
Paps of Jura

Sanaigmore

L. Gruinart

Sound of Islay

Port Askaig

Feolin

Gruinart

Ballygrant

A846

Craighouse

I s l a y

A846

Bridgend

Port Charlotte

L. Indaal

Bowmore

A847

A846

A8016

Ardtalla

Portnahaven

Rinns Pt.

Port Ellen

Ardbeg

The Oa

Mull of Oa

Macl

Rathlin I.

Mull of Kn

8km
5miles

Kilmory

Caolisport

Tighnabruaich

Kames

Colintraive

Dunoon

Innellan

A815

In

We

Ske

Lar

Port
Bannatyne

Rothesay

Ascot

A844

A83

Tarbert

W. Tarbert

B9024

Ardlamont Pt

K n a p d a

B
u
t
e

Kyles
of
Bute

Kennacraig

Whitehouse

B8001

Skipness

Claonaig

Summer
Only

Inchmarnock

Ardrey Road

A844

A846

Gt.
Cumbrae I.

Millport

33

52

Clachan

Crossaig

Lochranza

A841

S^d of Bute

Kilchattan

Lit.
Cumbrae I.

A78

B7

Tayinloan

Killean

Pirnmill

Sannox

Corrie

Goat Fell
2866

Seamill

Ardrossan

Carradale

Dippen

A841

B880

Brodick

F I R T

K
i
l
b
r
a
n
n
a
n
S
o
u
n
d

Saddell

B842

A r r a n

Lamlash

Holy I.

O F

Blackwaterfoot

A841

Whiting Bay

C L Y D

chenzie

Campbeltown

Davaar I.

Lagg

Pladda I.

Culzean Cas

Maidens

Turnberry

A77

uthend

Ailsa
Craig

Girvan

Clachan

A83

nbarr

n
t
y

r

Knap
d
a

W. Tarbert

a p d a

A83

Tighnabruaich

Kames

Colintraive

Dunoon

A770

A78

Po

Innellan

Inverkip

Tarbert

W. Tarbert

Port Bannatyne

Wemyss Bay

Skelmorlie

B8024

Kennacraig

Whitehouse

B8001

Ardlamont Pt.

Rothesay

Ascog

33

Gt. Cumbrae I.

Largs

Loc

52

Skipness

Inchmarnock

A844

A860

Millport

Fairlie

A760

Kilbi

lachan

Crossaig

Claonaig

(Summer Only)

Lochranza

Sd. of Bute

Kilchattan

Lit. Cumbrae I.

A78

Dalry

B781

B780

W. Kilbride

Kilwinn

rdale en

A841

Pirnmill

Sannox

Corrie

Goat Fell 2866

A841

B880

Brodick

Seamill

Ardrossan

Saltcoats

Steve

F I R T H

Kilbrannan Sound

A r r a n

Lamlash

Holy I.

Irvine Bay

O F

Tro

Blackwaterfoot

A841

Whiting Bay

C L Y D E

Pre

wn aar I.

Lagg

Pladda I.

A

Culzean Castle

Maybole

Maidens

Kirkoswald

Turnberry

A71

New Dai

Old Dailly

B741

Ailsa Craig

Girvan

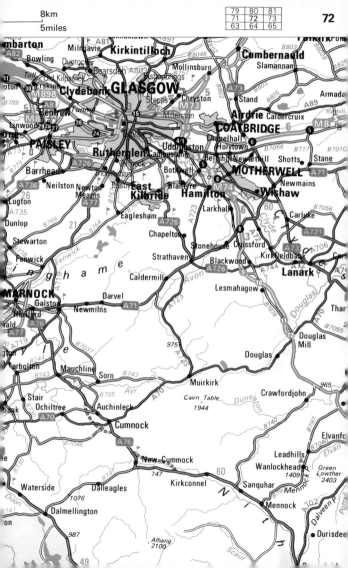

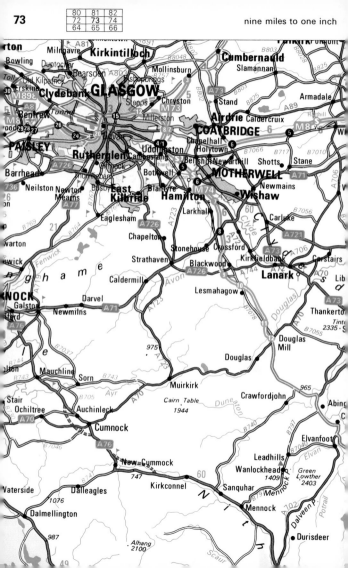

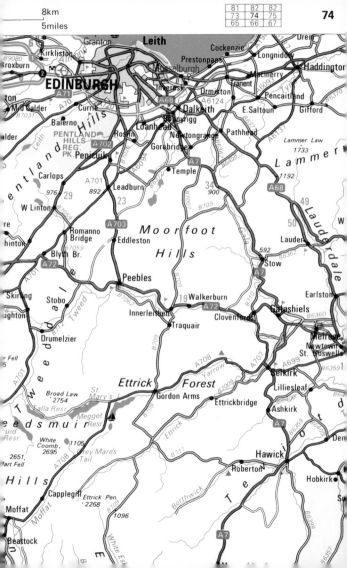

St. Abb's Hd.
St. Abb's
...0> *B6438*
...oldingham
Eyemouth
Burnmouth
Ayton
B6355
Chirnside
A6105
Whiteadder
Berwick-upon-Tweed
B6460
B6461
Spittal
A1167
Tweed
A1
A698
B6364
Norham
Ancroft
Beal
Holy Island
Duddo
Cornhill
on Tweed
Etal
B6353
Lowick
Budle Bay
Ford
30
Farne Islands
B6352
B6525
Belford
B6342
Bamburgh
...ork
B6351
Doddington
B6349
North
Sunderland
Seahouses
B1340
Beadnell
...rknewton
Chatton
B6348
Warenford
Wooler
A697
Beadnell Bay
Chillingham
The Cheviot
2676
46
B6347
Eglingham
B6347
Embleton
B1339
Ingram
Breamish
Aln
Longhoughton
Whittingham
Alnwick
A1
Lesbury
Alwinton
Edlingham
B6341
Alnmouth
Alnmouth Bay

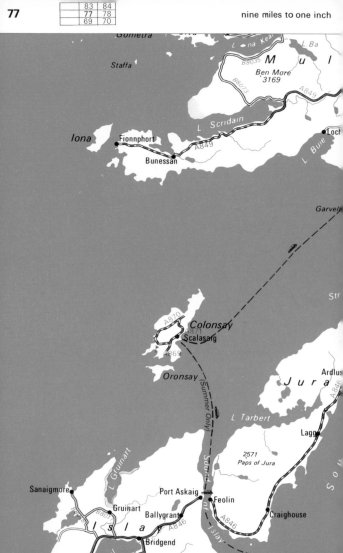

8km
5miles

Bridge of

Loch E

Glen Orchy

Connel

L Li

Lorn

A823

A85

Oban

Kerrera

A816

Bonawe

Taynuilt

Ben Cruachan
.3689

Pass of Brander

Loch Awe

Stronmilchan

B8077

42 Dalmally

Seil

Kilninver

Kilchrenan

Cladich

Portsonachan

Kilmelford

L Avich

Arduaine

Ardfern

37

B8003

A816

Ford

Glen Aray

Glen Shira

Inveraray

A83

St. Catherines

B828

A83

Lochgoilhead

Argyll's Bowling Green

Furnace

47

Strachur

Loch Fyne

Carrick Castle

Crarae

Newton

Kilmartin

Crinan

Cairnbaan

Lochgair

Lochmichael

Cowal

Loch Eck

Ardentinny

Coulport

Clynder

Rosneath

Cove

B8000

Tayvallich

Ardrishaig

A83

L Gilp

Otter Ferry

Glendaruel

Res.

Blairmore
Kilmun
Strone

Kilcre

Kilfinan

A8003

Sandbank

Kirn

Gourock

Dunoon

A885

Tighnabruaich

Colintraive

Kames

B u t e

Innellan

A815

A78

Tarbert

Kyles

A770

Inverkip

Wemyss Ba

W. Tarbert

Port Bannatyne

Skelmorlie

Kennacraig

Ardlamont Pt

Rothesay

Ascog

33

Whitehouse

B8001

Gt.

Knapdale

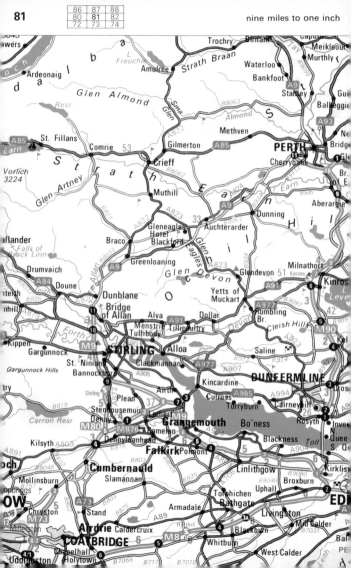

89	90
83	84
77	78

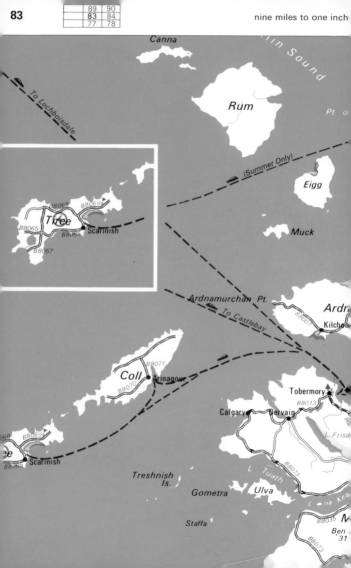

Canna

Rum

Sound

Pt o

To Lochboisdale

(Summer Only)

Eigg

B8068 B8069

Tiree

B8065

Muck

B8065

Scarinish

B8067

Ardnamurchan Pt.

Ard

To Castlebay

B8007

Kilcho

B8071

Coll Arinagour

Tobermory

B8070

B8073

Calgary Dervaig

B8069

L. Frisa

B8065 Scarinish

L. Tuath

Treshnish
Is.

B8073

L na Kea

Gometra Ulva

Staffa

B8035 M

Ben

31

B8073

8km
5miles

eangue

Airor

KNOYDART

Kinloch
Hourn

L. Clu

Glen
Glen

Sd of Sle

Ben Hourn

L. Quoich

L. Nevis

Mallaig

Morar

Murlaggan

B8005

L. Arkaig

A830

Arisaig

Loch Morar

Gai

L nan Uamh

L Eilt

47

Glenfinnan

B8004

Arisaig

A830

Corpach

Lochailort

A861

Loch Eil

L MORTA/A861

MOIDART

Loch Shiel

Fort
William

Kinlochmoidart

Polloch

Corran

L

Acharacle

N. Ballachulish

Salen

A861

Onich

Strontian

Glencoe

B8007

Kentallen

Gl

L Sunart

A884

Inversanda

Ballachulish

B8043

Loch Linnhe

A828

Bidean
nam
Bian

M o r v e r n

49

A p p i n

Glen

Claggan

Portnacroish

A884

Port
Appin

Lochaline

L Creran

Barcaldine

Ben Sta
3541

9

A828

L i s m o r e

Loch Etive

Craignure

Ben Cruachan
3689

nish

Lochdonhead

Connel

Bonawe

Pass of

A85

Oban

Taynuilt

Loch Awe

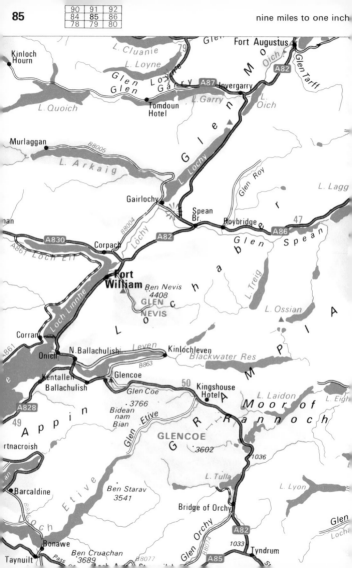

Kinloch
Hourn

L. Cluanie

L. Loyne

Glen Loyne

Glen Garry

A87 Invergarry

Fort Augustus

Glen Tarff

A82

L. Oich

Oich

Glen Moriston

L. Quoich

Tomdoun
Hotel

L. Garry

Glen

Murlaggan

B8005

L. Arkaig

Glen

L. Lochy

Glen Roy

L. Lagg

Gairlochy

B8004

Spean
Br.

Roybridge

A86

47

Glen Spean

A830

Corpach

A82

Lochy

nan

A861 Loch Eil

Fort
William

Ben Nevis
4408

GLEN
NEVIS

c

b

L. Treig

L. Ossian

h

a

M

P

I

A

Corran

Loch Linnhe

L

Leven

Kinlochleven

Blackwater Res

O

N. Ballachulish

Onich

B863

Kentallen

Glencoe

50

Kingshouse
Hotel

L. Laidon

L. Eigh

Ballachulish

Glen Coe

Moor of

A828

49

A p p i n

·3766
Bidean
nam
Bian

Glen Etive

GLENCOE

G

R

Rannoch

rtnacroish

·3602

1036

L. Lyon

Barcaldine

Ben Starav
3541

L. Tulla

Bridge of Orchy

Glen

Etive

Bonawe

Ben Cruachan
·3689

B8077

Glen Orchy

1033

A82

Tyndrum

A85

Taynuilt

Pass

8km
5miles

Brackburn

Bucksburn

Echt   Elrick

ABERDEEN

Lumphanan   *B9119*   *A944*

Garlogie   Cults

Torphins   *B993*   *B9125*   Bieldside   *B9077*

Kincardine   *A980*   *B977*   *A93*

59   O'Neil   Peterculter   Maryculter   *B9077*

Dee   *B993*   Hillside   Portlethen

arywell   *B976*   Camachmore   *A92*

Banchory   *B9077*   *A950*

Strachan   *B979*   Muchalls

W. of Feugh   h   Mowtie

t   Kerloch   *A957*

·1747

B974

W. of Dye   n

Cairn o' Mount   Stonehaven

·1488

sk N ESK   Auchinblae   *A94*

Fettercairn   *B966*   Roadside

B9120   *B967*

Edzell   *B974*   Laurencekirk   Inverbervie

The Mearns

Inchbare   53

B966   St. Cyrus

e   Marykirk   *A92*

Brechin   *A937*

A935   *A937*

Montrose

A933

A934

Friockheim   *Lunan B*

B965   Inverkeilor

B961   *A933*   Marywell

B9127

Arbroath

A92

Carnoustie

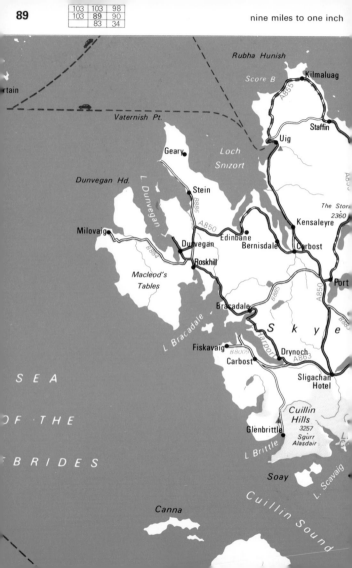

Rubha Hunish

Score B

Kilmaluag

Vaternish Pt.

Staffin

Uig

Geary

Loch
Snizort

Dunvegan Hd.

Stein

B886

Kensaleyre

The Store
2360

A850

Milovaig

Edinbane

Carbost

Dunvegan

Bernisdale

Roskhill

Port

B884

Macleod's
Tables

B885

Bracadale

S k y e

L. Bracadale

Fiskavaig

B8009

Drynoch

Carbost

A863

Sligachan
Hotel

SEA

O F T H E

Cuillin
Hills
3257
Sgurr
Alasdair

Glenbrittle

H E B R I D E S

L. Brittle

L. Scavaig

Soay

Canna

Cuillin Sound

Poolewe
STRATHNASHEALLAG
Fionn
Loch
Gair Loch
Gairloch
1110
B8056
Loch Maree
Hotel
A832
Slioch
3217
LOCH MAREE
Loch Torridon
Diabaig
TORRIDON
Ben Eighe
3309
Kinlochewe
Achnas
Inveralligin
3456
A890
815
L. a'Chroisc
Upr
L Torridon
Torridon
Shieldaig
Rona
L.
Damh
BEN DAMPH
APPLECROSS
Inner Sound
Beinn
Bhan
2936
Glen Carron
L.
Mor
Applecross
2054
Lochcarron
Achintee
Toscaig
Kishorn
L Kishorn
L Carron
Glen Carron
Ling
L. Mu
Plockton
Stromeferry
A890
Duirinish
Elchaig
Falls of
Glomach
Mam Soul
3862
L. Affr
Kyle of Lochalsh
A87
Dornie
KINTAIL
Kyleakin
L. Alsh
Inverinate
A850
Ben Attow
3383
Affric
ford
Breakish
Loch Duich
Invershiel
(Summer
Only)
Kylerhea
Glenelg
Shiel Bridge
Isle
Oronsay
A851
GLENELG
Glen Shiel
A87
Cluanie
889 Br
eangue
Arnisdale
Kinloch
Hourn
L. Clu
Loch Hourn
L. L
Airor
Glen
Glen
Sd of Sleat
KNOYDART

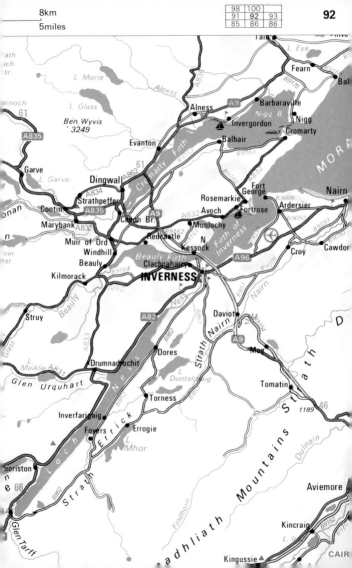

8km
5miles

L. Eye

Tain

Fearn

B9175

Bal

Strath
ich
sr.

L. Morie

Alness

B835

Barbaraville

Nigg B.

Nigg

Cromarty

arnoch

61

L. Glass

Ben Wyvis
·3249

Alness

Invergordon

Balbair

MORA

Evanton

B9163

A835

Garve

L. Garve

Cromarty Firth

61

Dingwall

A862

Fort
George

Nairn

Strathpeffer

A834

Rosemarkie

B9006

onan

Contin

A835

Avoch

Fortrose

Ardersier

B9092

B9091

B9090

Marybank

A832

Munlochy

Cawdor

n

Cluny Br.

A9

N.

Firth of
Inverness

Croy

rin
sr.

Muir of Ord

Redcastle

Kessock

A96

Windhill

Beauly Firth

B9164

Clachnaharry

Beauly

INVERNESS

Kilmorack

B802

Nairn

Beauly

Vess

Strath Nairn

Struy

A82

Daviot

A9

B851

A833

Meikle A831

Dores

L.
Duntelchaig

Moy

Drumnadrochit

Glen Urquhart

L. Ness

Torness

Tomatin

Glass

1189

46

Inverfarigaig

Errick

Foyers

Errogie

L.
Mhor

Strath
D

Dulnain

noriston

66

Loch Ness

Strath

B862

Findhorn

adhliath Mountains

Aviemore

Glen Tarff

Kincraig

B9152

L. In

Kingussie

CAIR

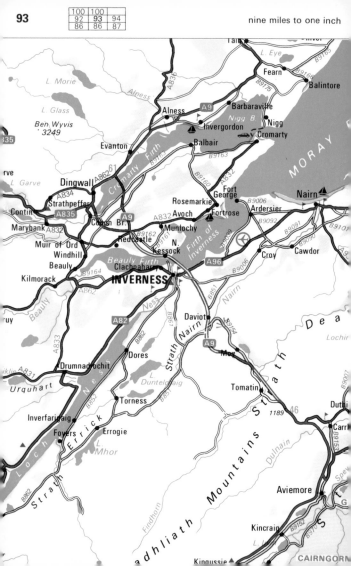

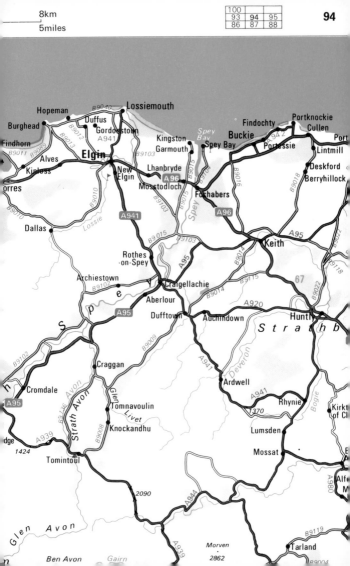

Hopeman
Lossiemouth
Burghead
Duffus
Gordonstown
B9040
B9012
A941
Findhorn
Kingston
Spey Bay
Findochty
Portknockie
Cullen
B9011
B9089
Garmouth
Spey Bay
Buckie
Port
Alves
Elgin
B9013
B9103
Portessie
Lintmill
orres
Kinloss
New Elgin
Lhanbryde
A96
B9014
Deskford
Berryhillock
B9018
Dallas
Mosstodloch
Fochabers
A96
Lossie
B9015
A95
Keith
A941
B9103
B9016
Rothes -on-Spey
B9103
A95
67
B9022
B9118
Archiestown
Craigellachie
B9014
B9115
B9102
Aberlour
A920
Huntly
Strathb
p e
A95
Dufftown
Auchindown
S
Craggan
B9009
Deveron
A941
Ardwell
A941
h
B9102
Cromdale
Glen
Livet
Rhynie
Kirkt of Cl
A95
Strath Avon
Tomnavoulin
T370
B9008
Knockandhu
Lumsden
Alf
dge
A939
1424
Mossat
M
Tomintoul
E
A980
2090
A944
B9119
Glen Avon
Morven 2862
Tarland
n
Ben Avon
Gairn
A939
B9004

Pennan
Rosehearty
Fraserburgh
Inverallochy
St. Combs
A92
New
Aberdour
Rathen
manhill
B9031
own
A98
Crimond
New
Pitsligo
Strichen
A952
Newbyth
B9093
18
Cuminestown
B9170
B u c h a n
Mintlaw
Ugie
Peterhead
New Deer
Old
Deer
A950
B9170
Clola
Burnhaven
43
A948
A92
A952
Methlick
Yth an
33
Cruden Bay
Cruden Bay
Tarves
B999
Ellon
B9955
A920
A920
Oldmeldrum
B9000
Collieston
A947
Newburgh
B977
Newmachar
A92
To Lerwick & Stromness
Kintore
Dyce
A96
Blackburn
B9119
Bucksburn
Elrick
ABERDEEN
Garlogie
A944
Cults

Gair Loch

1088

Inverasdale
Melvaig

Cove

Poolewe

B8057

Gairloch

B8021

Loch Maree

Loch Ewe

Inverewe

Aultbea

Mellon
Charles
Laide

A832

STRATHNASHEALLAG

Fionn
Loch

L. na
Sealga

An Teallach
· 3483

A832

Gruinard

Gruinard B

Gruinard I.

Badluachrach

Loch Broom

Summer Isles

Tanera More

Achiltibuie

L Lurgain

Enard
Bay

Inverkirkaig

Suilven
2399

Caniso
2779

Stac Polly
2009

INVERPOLLY

L Veyatie

Dundonnell

Falls of
Measach

L. a'
Braoin

A835

Ardmair

Ullapool

Ardcharnich

A835

Strathkanaird

A835

810

Elphin

Sionascaig

Cromalt

A837

44

Ledmore Lo.

Inchnadamph
3273
Ben More Assynt

A837

· Sgurr Mor
3637

Benn Dearg
3547

755

Strath
Vaich
Resr.

Gleann Mor

55

Oykel Br.

Oykel

Strath Cassley

Glen Cassley

Loch

L a'
Glasqarnoch

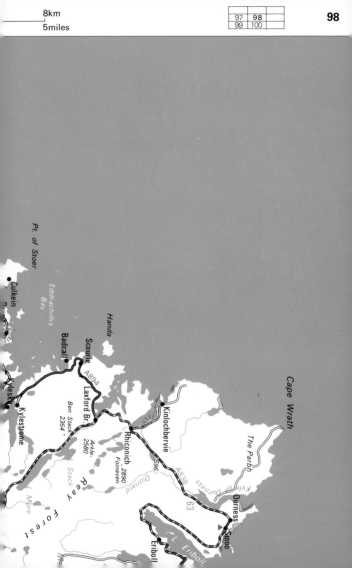

Pt. of Stoer

Culkein

Eddrachillis Bay

Handa

Badcall

Scourie

A894

Laxford Br.

Ben Stack 2364

Arkle 2580

Rhiconich

Foinaven 2890

Ben Mhor

Kinlochbervie

Cape Wrath

The Parbh

Kyle of Durness

Durness

A838

A838

63

Smoo

Kylesku

Kylestrome

L. More

Stack

Reay Forest

Dionard

L. Eriboll

Eriboll

8km
5miles

Smoo
L. Eriboll
Eriboll
Ben
Hope
3040
741
A838
Meadie
Melness
Altnaharra
A836
Ben
Loyal
2504
Tongue
L. Naver
Loch Loyal
Borgie
Skerray
Farr
Strath Naver
Armadale
Naver
B871
Bettyhill
A836
44
Strathy
Strathy Pt.
L. nan
Cuinne
Strathy
Melvich
Loch Baddanloch
Forsinard
Hotel
Portskerra
563
Strath Halladale
Golval
A897
Trantlebeg
Reay
Dounreay
Trantlebeg
A836
L. Calder
Forss
Scrabster
Dunbeath
Thurso
To Stromness
L.
Watten
A882
Halkirk
Thurso
B870
B874
Castletown
A836
Myhster
A895
21
A836
Roadside
Dunnet
Latheron
Achav
Lyb
B855
Dunnet H

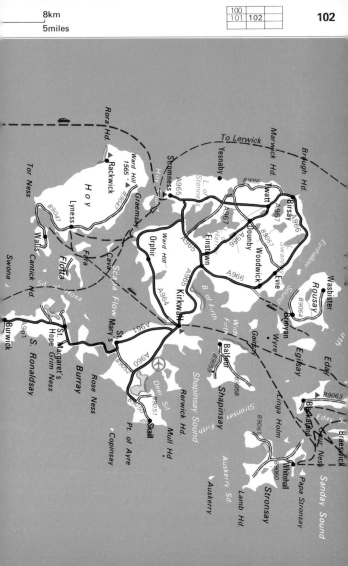

Butt of Lew

Port of Ness

Galson

Borve

Barvas

A 858

Carloway

Stornoway

Broad B. Tiumpa

Portnagu

Eye

Peninsul

Stornoway Harb.

North Tolsta

Tolsta He

A 857

Eriskdy

Sound of Barra

Barra A 888

Castlebay

Vatersay

Sandray

Pabbay

Berneray

Mingulay

Barra Hd.

Gallan Hd. L. Roag Gt.

Uig Bernera

Ardroil Sands

Callanish

Garynahine

A 859

Balallan

L. Erisort

L. Langavat

Resort

L E W I S

Lemreway

Loch L. Shell

Seaforth

Nort

Mi

Scarp

Clisham

2622

W. Loch Tarbert

Tarbert

Taransay

Scalpay

Shiant Is.

Toe Hd.

A 859

Loch Tarbert

Leverburgh Harris

Pabbay

Berneray

Sound of Harris

Rodel

Rubha Hunish

Duntulm Kilmaluag

Haskeir

Is.

Staffin

North Uist Lochmaddy

Vaternish

Pt.

Uig

A 855

Clachan

L. Eport

Carinish

Monach Is.

Grimsay

Gramisdale

Ronay

Benbecula

Creagorry

Carnan

L Bagh nam Faoileann

L. Skiport

**South

Uist**

Beinn

Mhor

2034

L. Eynort

Daliburgh

Lochboisdale

Kilbride

Ludag

Eriskay

Sound of Barra

Dunvegan Hd.

Stein

L. Dunvegan

L. Pooltiel

Milovaig

Dunvegan

Loch

Snizort

Bernisdale

Skeabost

The Storr

2358

S

A 850

Portree

Bracadale

Struan

L. Bracadale

Carbost

Sligachan

L. Eynort

Cuillin

3257

Hills

L. Brittle

Cuillin Sound

Sooy

L. Scavaig

Elg

Canna

Sd. of Canna

Rum

Pt. of Sle

O U T E R   H E B R I D E S

Little Mi

Loch of the

Sd. of Raasa

Sound of

L. Cor

Arn

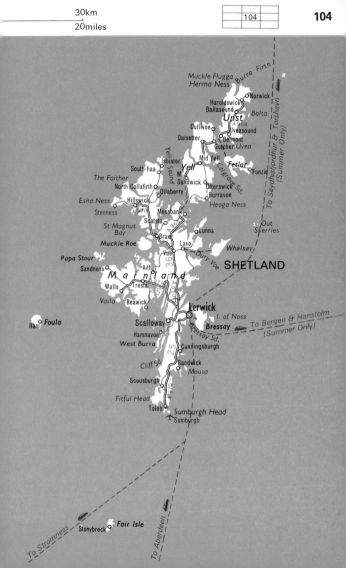

30km
20miles

Muckle Flugga
Herma Ness

Norwick

Haroldswick
Baltasound
Unst
Balta
Burra Firth

Cullivoe

Uyeasound
Belmont
Daisetter
Gutcher Uyea

A 968

To Seydhisfjordhur & Torshavn
(Summer Only)

Mid Yell
Fetlar
Isbister
Yell
Funzie
South-haa
W.
Sandwick
The Faither
Otterswick
North Collafirth
Ollaberry
Burravoe
Yell Sound
Colgrave Sd.

Esha Ness
Hillswick
Heoga Ness
Stenness

St Magnus
Bay
Mossbank
Scatsta
Out
Skerries

Muckle Roe
Brae

Lunna

Papa Stour
Voe
Laxo
Whalsay

Sandness
Aith
Dury Voe
SHETLAND

Mainland

Walls
Tresta

Vaila
Reawick

Lerwick

I. of Noss

Ham
Foula
Bressay
To Bergen & Hanstolm
(Summer Only)
Bressay Sd.

Scalloway
Hamnavoe
Cunningsburgh
West Burra

Cliff Sd.
Sandwick
Mousa

Scousburgh

Fitful Head
Tolob

Sumburgh Head
Sumburgh

To Stromness

Stonybreck
Fair Isle

To Aberdeen

Index

This index comprises a selection of names and locations of towns and villages based on population, route importance, and postal significance. The reference number refers to the page, and the letter refers to the section of the map in which the index entry can be found, as divided into **a**, **b**, **c**, and **d** thus:

a	b
c	d

A

Abbey St.Bathans	75b	Adderbury	29c
Abbey Town	65d	Addington	19d
Abbotsbury	8c	Adwick-le-Street	48a
Aberaeron	25a	Ainsdale	51d
Aberargie	81b	Aintree	45b
Abercarn	24d	Aird of Sleat	84a
Aberchirder	95b	Airdrie	73b
Aberdare	24a	Airth	81c
Aberdaron	43c	Albrighton	35d
Aberdeen	96c	Alcester	28a
Aberdour	81d	Aldbrough	56c
Aberdyfi	33c	Aldeburgh	41d
Aberedw	26a	Alderley Edge	46b
Aberfeldy	86d	Alderminster	28b
Aberffraw	43b	Aldershot	11a
Abergavenny	24b	Alexandria	79d
Abergele	44b	Alford (Grampian)	95d
Abergwynfi	24a	Alford (Lincs)	50c
Aberlady	82c	Alfreton	48c
Aberllefenni	33c	Alfriston	12c
Aberlour	94a	Alkham	14a
Abernethy	81b	Allanby	65d
Aberporth	22a	Allenheads	67d
Abersoch	43d	Allesley	28b
Abertillery	24b	Allgreave	47c
Aberystwyth	25b	Alloa	80d
Abingdon	17b	Almondsbury	15b
Abington	73d	Alness	93a
Aboyne	88a	Alnmouth	68a
Accrington	52c	Alnwick	68a
Acharacle	84c	Alpheton	32a
Acharn	86c	Alresford	10a
Achavanich	101a	Alrewas	36a
Achiltibuie	97b	Alston	66d
Achintree	90b	Alston Cross	28c
Achnasheen	91b	Altassmore	99b
Acklington	68a	Altnaharra	100a
Acock's Green	36c	Alton	10b
Acomb	54b	Altrincham	46b
Acton Turville	16a	Alva	81c

Alvanley	46c	Arundel	11d
Alvaston	36b	Ascot	18d
Alvechurch	28a	Asfordby	37b
Alyth	87d	Ash	14a
Amble	68a	Ashbourne	36a
Ambleside	58c	Ashburton	4a
Amersham	18a	Ashby	49b
Amesbury	9b	Ashby de la Zouch	36b
Amlwch	43b	Ashford (Kent)	13b
Ammanford	23b	Ashington	68a
Ampleforth	61d	Ashstead	19d
Ampthill	30c	Ashton Keynes	16b
Amulree	80b	Ashton-under-Lyne	47a
Ancaster	38a	Ashton-in-Makerfield	46a
Ancroft	76c	Askham	57c
Andover	9b	Aspatria	65d
Andoversford	28c	Aston	48a
Annan	65d	Atherstone	36c
Annbank	72c	Atherton	46a
Anstruther	82b	Attleborough	42a
Appleby	58b	Atwick	56a
Applecross	90a	Atworth	16c
Appledore (Devon)	5b	Auchencairn	64c
Appledore (Kent)	13d	Auchentiber	72a
Arbroath	88b	Auchinblae	88a
Archiestown	94a	Auchindown	95a
Ardarroch	90c	Auchinleck	73c
Ardbeg	69b	Auchterarder	81b
Ardcharnich	97c	Auchtermuchty	82a
Ardentinny	79d	Aultbea	97a
Ardeonaig	80a	Aviemore	93d
Ardersier	93b	Avoch	93d
Ardfern	78a	Avonmouth	15b
Ardgay	99c	Axbridge	15c
Ardlui	79b	Axminster	7c
Ardlussa	77d	Aylesbury	30c
Ardmair	97b	Aylesham	14a
Ardminish	70a	Aylsham	40a
Ardrishaig	78c	Aynho	29c
Ardrossan	71b	Ayr	71c
Ardtalla	69b	Aysgarth	59d
Arduaine	78a	Ayton	76a
Arinagour	83c		
Arisaig	84a	**B**	
Armadale (Skye)	84a		
Armadale (Highland)	100b	Backaland	101d
Arncliffe	52b	Bacup	52d
Arnesby	37c	Badcall	98c
Arnisdale	90d	Badluachrach	97a
Arnprior	80c	Bagby	61d
Arnside	51b	Bagshot	18c
Arrochar	79d	Bakewell	47d
Arthog	33a	Bala	44c

Balallan	103b	Basingstoke	17d
Balbair	93a	Baslow	47d
Balbeggie	81b	Bath	15d
Balcombe	12a	Bathgate	73b
Baldock	30d	Batley	54c
Balerno	74a	Battle	13c
Balfour	101c	Battlefield	35a
Balintore	93b	Baumber	50c
Ballachulish	85c	Bawtry	48b
Ballantrae	63a	Baynards Green	29d
Ballater	87b	Beaconsfield	18a
Ballaugh	51c	Beadnell	76d
Ballinluig	86d	Beal	76c
Ballygrant	69b	Beaminster	8c
Balmaha	79d	Beattock	65b
Balmullo	82a	Beaulieu	9d
Balsham	31b	Beauly	92a
Baltasound	104b	Beaumaris	44a
Bamber Bridge	52c	Bebington	45b
Bamburgh	76d	Beccles	42c
Bampton	7a	Beckingham	49a
Banbury	29c	Bedale	60c
Banchory	28a	Bedford	30b
Banff	95b	Bedlington	68c
Bangor	44a	Bedworth	36d
Bannockburn	81c	Beer	7d
Banstead	19c	Beeston	37a
Barbaraville	93b	Beith	71b
Barcaldine	79a	Belford	76d
Bardon Mill	67d	Bellingham	67b
Bardsea	51b	Bellochantuy	70c
Bargoed	24b	Bellshill	73a
Bargrennan	63b	Belmont	52c
Barking	19b	Belper	48c
Barlborough	48c	Belsay	68a
Barmouth	33a	Bembridge	10c
Barnard Castle	60a	Benson	17b
Barnet	19a	Bentley	48a
Barnoldswick	53a	Bere Regis	8d
Barnsley	48a	Berkeley	15b
Barnstaple	6a	Berkhamsted	18a
Barr	63b	Bernisdale	89b
Barrhead	72a	Berriedale	99b
Barrhill	63b	Berryhillock	95b
Barrow	56c	Berwick-upon-Tweed	76a
Barrow-in-Furness	51a	Bethesda	44a
Barry	24d	Bettyhill	100b
Barton (Humberside)	56c	Betws-y-Coed	44b
Barton (Bedfordshire)	30c	Beulah	26a
Barton Mills	31b	Beverley	56c
Barvas	103b	Bewdley	27b
Baschurch	34b	Bexhill-on-Sea	13d
Basildon	20a	Bexley	19b

Bicester	29d	Blagdon (Somerset)	7
Bickley Moss	46c	Blair Atholl	86
Biddendon	13d	Blairgowrie	87
Biddulph	47c	Blakeney (Norfolk)	40
Bideford	5b	Blakeney (Glos)	15
Bidford	28a	Blakenham	32
Bigbury on Sea	3d	Blanchland	67
Biggar	74c	Blandford Forum	8
Biggleswade	30b	Blankney	49
Bilbister	101b	Blantyre	73
Billericay	20a	Blaydon	68
Billesdon	37d	Blean	14
Billingborough	38a	Bletchingley	12
Billingshurst	11b	Blewbury	17
Bilston	35d	Blindley Heath	12
Bingham	37b	Blofield	42
Bingley	53d	Bloxwich	36
Binley	29a	Blubberhouses	53
Birchington	14b	Blyth (Northumberland)	68
Birdlip	28c	Blyth Bridge	74
Birgham	75d	Blythburgh	41
Birkenhead	45b	Blyton	49
Birmingham	36c	Boat of Garton	93
Birnam	87c	Bodfari	45
Birsay	101d	Bodmin	2
Birtley	68c	Bognor Regis	11
Bishop Auckland	60a	Boldon	68
Bishopbriggs	73a	Boldre	9
Bishop Burton	55d	Bollington	47
Bishops Castle	34c	Bolton	46
Bishop's Caundle	8a	Bolventor	2
Bishop's Cleeve	28c	Bonar Bridge	99
Bishops Lydeard	7b	Boncath	22
Bishop's Stortford	31c	Bonchester Bridge	75
Bishops Waltham	10a	Bo'ness	81
Bisley	18c	Bonhill	79
Bitterne	10a	Bonnyrigg	74
Blaby	37c	Boothby Pagnell	38
Blackbrook	35b	Bootle (Cumbria)	57
Blackburn	52c	Bootle (Merseyside)	45
Blackford	81a	Boreland	65
Blackmoor Gate	6a	Borough Green	20
Blackness	81d	Boroughbridge	54
Blackpool	51d	Borrowdale	57
Blackwaterfoot	70c	Borth	33
Blackwood (S'clyde)	73b	Borve	103
Blackwood (Gwent)	24d	Boscastle	5
Bladnoch	64c	Bosley	47
Blaenau Ffestiniog	44c	Boston	50
Blaenavon	24b	Botesdale	41
Blaenporth	22a	Bothwell	73
Blaenrhondda	24a	Botley (Oxon)	17
Blagdon (Avon)	15d	Botley (Hants)	10

Bourne	38a	Bridge of Weir	71b
Bournemouth	9c	Bridgend (Strathclyde)	69a
Bovey Tracey	4a	Bridgend (Mid Glamorgan)	24c
Bow	4a	Bridgnorth	35d
Bow Street	33c	Bridgwater	7b
Bowes	59b	Bridlington	56a
Bowland Bridge	58c	Bridport	8c
Bowling	80c	Brierley Hill	35d
Bowmore	69a	Brigg	49b
Bowness	58c	Brighouse	53d
Box	16c	Brighstone	10c
Bracadale	89d	Brightling	13c
Bracebridge	49d	Brightlingsea	32d
Brackley	29d	Brighton	12c
Bracknell	18c	Brinkley	31b
Braco	80b	Brinkworth	16a
Bradfield	17d	Brinyan	101d
Bradford	53d	Brisley	40a
Bradford-on-Avon	16c	Bristol	15b
Bradwell on Sea	20b	Briton Ferry	23d
Braemar	87a	Brixham	4c
Brailsford	36a	Brixworth	29b
Braintree	31d	Broad Chalke	9a
Bramdean	10a	Broad Clyst	7c
Bramham	54c	Broad Haven	21d
Bramley	11b	Broad Hinton	16b
Brampton (Cambs)	30b	Broadford	90c
Brampton (Cumbria)	66c	Broadstairs	14b
Brancaster	39b	Broadway	28d
Brancepeth	60a	Broadwey	8c
Brandesburton	56a	Broadwindsor	7d
Brandon (Durham)	60a	Brockenhurst	9d
Brandon (Suffolk)	39d	Brodick	70b
Branston	49d	Bromborough	45b
Brant Broughton	49d	Bromley	19d
Braunton	5b	Brompton	62d
Brayford	6a	Bromsgrove	28a
Breage	1d	Bromyard	27b
Breakish	90c	Bronnant	25b
Bream	15b	Brookland	13d
Brechin	88c	Brora	99b
Brecon	24a	Broseley	35c
Brede	13d	Brotton	62a
Bredhurst	20c	Brough	58b
Brentford	19a	Broughton (Borders)	74c
Brentwood	19b	Broughton (Cumbria)	57d
Brenzett	13d	Brownhills	36c
Bridge of Alford	95d	Broxburn	74a
Bridge of Allan	81c	Bruton	8a
Bridge of Cally	87c	Bryn-amman	25d
Bridge of Earn	81b	Bryn-crug	33c
Bridge of Gairn	87b	Bryneglwys	45c
Bridge of Orchy	85d	Brynmawr	24b

Bubwith	55d
Buckden	30b
Buckfastleigh	4c
Buckhaven	82c
Buckie	94b
Buckingham	29d
Buckley	45d
Bucks Green	11b
Bucksburn	88b
Bude	5c
Budleigh Salterton	7c
Builth Wells	26a
Bulwick	38c
Bunessan	77a
Bungay	42c
Bunny	37a
Buntingford	31c
Bures	32c
Burford	28d
Burgess Hill	12c
Burgh le Marsh	50d
Burghead	94a
Burley	53c
Burnham	15c
Burnham Market	39b
Burnham on Crouch	20b
Burnhaven	96b
Burniston	62d
Burnley	52d
Burnmouth	76a
Burnopfield	68c
Burnsall	53b
Burntisland	82c
Burravoe	104b
Burry Port	22d
Burscough Bridge	45b
Burslem	46d
Burton	49d
Burton Agnes	56a
Burton Leonard	54a
Burton in Kendal	58c
Burton in Lonsdale	52a
Burton upon Trent	36a
Burwash	13c
Burwell (Cambs)	31b
Burwell (Lincs)	50a
Burwick	101c
Bury	46b
Bury St Edmonds	32a
Buttermere	57b
Buttington	34a
Buxton	47d
Byfleet	18d

Byrness	66b
Bythorne	30a

C

Cadbury	4a
Cadnam	9b
Caenby Corner	49b
Caerleon	15a
Caernarfon	43b
Caerphilly	24d
Caersws	34c
Caerwent	15a
Cairnbaan	78c
Cairnryan	63a
Caister-on-Sea	42d
Caistor	49b
Caldbeck	66c
Caldecott	37d
Calder Bridge	57c
Caldercruix	72b
Caldicot	15b
Caldwell	60a
Calgary	83d
Callander	80a
Callanish	103b
Callington	3b
Calne	16c
Calveley	46c
Calver	47d
Camberley	18c
Camborne	1d
Cambridge	31a
Camelford	5c
Cammachmore	88b
Campbeltown	70c
Camptown	67a
Cannich	92c
Cannington	7b
Cannock	35d
Canonbie	66a
Canterbury	14a
Canvey	20a
Capel	11b
Capenhurst	45d
Capplegill	74c
Caputh	87c
Carbis Bay	1d
Carbost	89b
Cardiff	24d
Cardigan	22a
Carinish	103c
Carisbrooke	10c

Carlisle	66c	Checkley	36a
Carlops	74a	Cheddar	15c
Carlton on Trent	48d	Chelmsford	20a
Carluke	73b	Cheltenham	28c
Carmarthen	22b	Chepstow	15b
Carnforth	51b	Cheriton	10a
Carno	33d	Chertsey	18d
Carnoustie	82b	Chesham	18b
Carnwath	73b	Cheshunt	19b
Carradale	70a	Chessell	10c
Carrbridge	93d	Chester	45d
Carrick Castle	78d	Chester-le-Street	68c
Carronbridge	65a	Chesterfield	48c
Carsphairn	64a	Chew Stoke	15d
Carstairs	73b	Chicheley	30a
Carter Bar	67a	Chichester	11c
Casterton	58c	Chicklade	9a
Castlebay	103a	Chiddingfold	11a
Castle Cary	98a	Chideock	7d
Castle Douglas	64d	Chigwell	19b
Castleford	54c	Chilham	14a
Castle Hedingham	32c	Chillingham	76c
Castle Kennedy	63d	Chilton Foliat	17c
Castle Rising	39b	Chinnor	18a
Castleside	68c	Chippenham	16a
Castleton (Derbys)	47b	Chipping Camden	28d
Castleton (N.Yorks)	62b	Chipping Norton	28d
Castletown	51c	Chipping Ongar	19b
Caterham	19a	Chipping Sodbury	15b
Catterick	60c	Chirnside	76a
Cavendish	32a	Chiseldon	16b
Cawdor	93b	Chiselhurst	19d
Caxton	31a	Chobham	18c
Cemaes Bay	43b	Chorley	52c
Ceres	82a	Christchurch	9d
Cerne Abbas	8c	Chryston	72b
Chagford	4a	Chudleigh	4a
Chale	10c	Chulmleigh	6c
Chalfont St. Giles	18a	Church Stretton	34d
Chandler's Ford	10a	Churchill	15c
Chapel Allerton	54c	Churston Ferrers	4c
Chapel en le Frith	47b	Cinderford	27d
Chapel St.Leonards	50d	Cirencester	16a
Chard	7b	Clachnaharry	92b
Charlbury	29c	Clackmannan	80d
Charlton Kings	28c	Clacton-on-Sea	32d
Charlwood	11b	Clanfield	10b
Charmouth	7d	Claonaig	70a
Chatham	20c	Clapham	52a
Chatteris	38d	Clarencefield	65d
Chatton	76c	Clashmore	99a
Cheadle (Staffs)	36a	Clashnessie	98a
Cheadle (Grtr Manchester)	46b	Clawton	5d

Clay Cross	48c	Connel	78a
Claydon	41a	Conon Bridge	92a
Clayton-le-Moors	52d	Consett	68c
Cleator	57a	Contin	92a
Cleehill	27b	Conwy	44a
Cleethorpes	50a	Conwyl Elfed	22a
Cleobury Mortimer	27b	Cooden	13c
Clevedon	15c	Cookham	18a
Cleveleys	51d	Coolham	11b
Clitheroe	52c	Coombe Bissett	9b
Cloughton	62d	Coombe Martin	6c
Clova	87b	Copplestone	6c
Clovelly	5b	Corbridge	67d
Clovenfords	75c	Corby	37d
Clun	34c	Corfe Castle	9c
Clydebank	72a	Corhampton	10a
Clynder	79d	Cornhill (Grampian)	95b
Clyst Honiton	7c	Cornhill on Tweed	76c
Coalville	36b	Cornwood	3d
Coatbridge	73a	Corpach	85a
Cobham (Surrey)	18d	Corran	84d
Cobham (Kent)	20c	Corrie Common	65b
Cockburnspath	75b	Corringham	49a
Cockenzie	82c	Corsham	16c
Cockermouth	57b	Corston	16a
Codicote	30d	Corwen	34a
Coggleshall	32c	Cosham	10a
Colchester	32c	Coshieville	86c
Cold Ashton	15d	Cotherstone	59b
Coldingham	76a	Cottenham	31a
Cold Norton	20a	Cottingham	56c
Coldstream	76c	Coupar Angus	87d
Coleford (Glos)	15b	Cove	79d
Coleshill	36c	Coventry	29a
Colintraive	78d	Coverack	2c
Collieston	96d	Cowbridge	24c
Collingham (W.Yorks)	54a	Cowdenbeath	81d
Collingham (Notts)	49c	Cowes	10c
Colmonell	63b	Cowfold	11b
Colnbrook	18b	Coxhoe	61a
Colne	52d	Coychurch	24c
Colpy	95d	Crackleybank	35b
Colsterworth	37b	Craigellachie	94b
Coltishall	42b	Craighouse	69b
Colwyn Bay	44b	Craignure	78a
Colyford	7d	Craigton	87d
Comrie	80b	Crail	82b
Congleton	46d	Cramlington	68c
Congresbury	15c	Cranborne	9a
Coningsby	50c	Cranbrook	13d
Conisbrough	48a	Cranford St.John	30a
Coniston	57d	Cranleigh	11b
Connah's Quay	45d	Cranswick	56a

Crathorne	61d	Cullompton	7a
Craven Arms	34d	Culmstock	7a
Crawford	73d	Culross	81d
Crawfordjohn	73d	Cults	88b
Crawley	11b	Cumbernauld	73b
Cray	24a	Cuminestown	96a
Creagorry	103c	Cumnock	72c
Credenhill	27c	Cunningsburgh	104d
Crediton	4a	Cupar	82a
Creetown	64c	Currie	74a
Cresselly	21d	Cury Cross	1d
Crewe	46c	Cwmbran	15a
Crewkerne	7b		
Crianlarich	79b	**D**	
Cribyn	25a		
Criccieth	43d	Dagenham	19b
Crickhowell	26d	Dalbeattie	64d
Cricklade	16b	Dale	21d
Crieff	80b	Daliburgh	103c
Crinan	78c	Dalkeith	74b
Crockernwell	4a	Dallas	94a
Crockham Hill	12a	Dalleagles	72c
Croft	61c	Dalmally	78b
Cromarty	93b	Dalmellington	72c
Cromdale	94c	Dalry (D & G)	64a
Cromer	40b	Dalry (S'clyde)	71b
Cromford	48a	Dalsetter	104b
Crook	60a	Dalton	51b
Crosby (Merseyside)	45b	Dalwhinnie	86a
Crosby (I.of W.)	51c	Danbury	20a
Crosby Ravensworth	58b	Daresbury	46a
Croshills	53b	Darfield	48a
Cross Hands	23b	Darlington	60a
Cross-Keys	24d	Dartford	19b
Crossaig	70a	Dartmeet	4a
Crosshill	71d	Dartmouth	4c
Crowborough	12a	Darvel	72a
Crowcombe	7a	Darwen	52c
Crowland	38a	Dava	94c
Crowle	55d	Daventry	29b
Crowthorne	18c	Davidstow	5c
Croxton Kerrial	37b	Daviot	93b
Croydon	19d	Dawley	35d
Cruden Bay	96d	Dawlish	4b
Crudgington	35a	Deal	14b
Crudwell	16a	Debenham	41b
Crymmych	22a	Deddington	29c
Crynant	23b	Deeping St.Nicholas	38a
Cuckfield	12a	Denbigh	45c
Cudworth	48a	Denby Dale	47b
Culgaith	59a	Denham	18b
Culkein	98a	Denholm	75d
Cullen	95b	Dennington	41b

Denny	80d	Drumnadrochit	92c
Denton	47a	Drumnaich	80a
Derby	36b	Drynoch	89c
Dereham	40a	Duddo	76c
Dersingham	39b	Dudley	35c
Dervaig	83d	Duffield	36b
Deskford	95b	Dufftown	95a
Devizes	16c	Duffus	94a
Devonport	3d	Duirnish	90c
Dewsbury	54c	Dulnain Bridge	94c
Diabaig	90a	Dulverton	6b
Dicker	12c	Dumbarton	79d
Didcot	17b	Dumfries	65a
Didmarton	16a	Dunbar	75b
Dingwall	92a	Dunbeath	100b
Dinnet	87b	Dunblane	80b
Dirleton	82d	Dunbridge	9b
Diss	32b	Dundee	82a
Distington	57a	Dundonald	72a
Ditton Priors	35c	Dundrennan	64d
Docking	39b	Dunfermline	81d
Docklow	27b	Dunholme	49b
Doddington	38d	Dunkeld	86d
Dolbenmaen	43d	Dunlop	72a
Dolgellau	33a	Dunnet	101b
Dollar	81d	Dunning	81b
Dolphinton	74a	Dunoon	78d
Dolwyddelan	44c	Duns	75b
Doncaster	48b	Dunstable	30c
Donington (Lincs)	38a	Dunster	7a
Dorchester (Dorset)	8c	Dunsyre	74a
Dorchester (Oxon)	17b	Dunvegan	89c
Dores	93c	Dunwich	41d
Dorking	11b	Durham	60a
Dornie	90d	Durness	98d
Dornoch	99a	Dursley	16a
Dorrington	34d	Durston	7b
Douglas (Strathclyde)	73d	Durweston	8b
Douglas (I.of M.)	51c	Duthil	93d
Dounby	101d	Dyce	96c
Doune	80d	Dykehead	87b
Dounreay	100d	Dymchurch	14c
Dover	14b	Dymock	27d
Dowally	86d	Dysart	82c
Downham Market	39c		
Downton	9b	**E**	
Draycott	36a		
Drayton	42b	Eaglesham	73a
Drem	82d	Eaglesham	72a
Droitwich	28a	Earby	53a
Dronfield	48b	Earls Colne	32c
Drumbeg	98a	Earlston	75d
Drummore	63d	Easdale	78a

asebourne	11a	Eltham	19d
asington	68d	Elton	38c
ast Barkwith	50a	Elvanfoot	73d
ast Bridgford	37b	Elvington	55a
astbourne	12d	Elworthy	7a
ast Cowes	10c	Ely	31b
astchurch	20d	Embleton	76d
astdean	12d	Emsworth	10b
ast Grinstead	12a	Enfield	19b
ast Hoathley	12c	Epping	19b
ast Horsley	11b	Epsom	19c
asthampstead	18c	Epworth	49a
asthampton	18c	Eriboll	98d
ast Kilbride	72b	Errogie	92c
astleigh	10a	Erwood	26c
ast Linton	82d	Esher	18d
ast Lulworth	8d	Etal	76c
ast Markham	49c	Ettington	28b
ast Retford	48b	Ettrickbridge End	75c
astriggs	65d	Evanton	92a
astry	14b	Evelix	99a
ast Wemyss	82c	Evercreech	8a
astwood	48c	Everingham	55d
aton Socon	30b	Evesham	28c
bbw Vale	24b	Ewenny	24c
bchester	68c	Ewhurst	11b
cclefechan	65b	Exbourne	3b
ccleshall	35b	Exeter	4b
cht	96c	Exford	6b
ckington	48a	Exminster	4a
dderton	99a	Exmouth	4b
ddlestone	74a	Eye	41b
denbridge	12a	Eyemouth	76a
dgcumbe	1d	Eynsford	19d
dgware	19a	Eynsham	17b
dinbane	89b		
dinburgh	74a	**F**	
dzell	88c		
gham	18d	Fairford	16b
glingham	76d	Fairlie	71b
gremont	57a	Fakenham	39b
ilean Iarmain	90c	Falkirk	80d
lgin	94a	Falkland	82a
lgol	89d	Falmer	12c
lie	82c	Falmouth	2c
lland	53d	Falstone	66b
llesmere	34b	Fangfoss	55b
llesmere Port	45b	Fareham	10a
llon	96c	Faringdon	17a
lphin	97d	Farnborough (London)	19d
lrick	96c	Farnborough (Hants)	11a
lstow	30a	Farndon	45d
lstree	19a	Farnham	11a

Farnham Royal	18a	Folkingham	38a
Farnworth	46a	Fontmell Magna	8b
Faversham	13b	Ford	76c
Fawley	10c	Fordham	31b
Fazeley	36c	Fordingbridge	9b
Fearn	93b	Forest Row	12a
Fearnan	86c	Forfar	87c
Featherstone	54c	Formby	45b
Felbridge	12a	Fornham St.Martin	32a
Felixstowe	41c	Forres	94a
Felling	68c	Fort Augustus	92c
Felpham	11c	Fort George	93b
Felton	68a	Fort William	85a
Feltwell	39d	Fortinghall	86c
Fenstanton	31a	Fortrose	93b
Fenwick	72a	Fortuneswell	8c
Feolin	69b	Four Oaks	36c
Ferndown	9c	Fovant	9a
Fernhurst	11a	Fowey	2b
Ferrybridge	54c	Foxholes	56a
Ferryhill	60a	Foyers	92c
Ferryside	22d	Fraddon	2a
Fettercairn	88a	Framlingham	41b
Ffestiniog	44c	Frant	13c
Ffostrasol	22b	Fraserburgh	96b
Filby	42d	Freshwater	9c
Filey	56a	Fressingfield	41b
Filton	15b	Freswick	101c
Finborough	41b	Fridaythorpe	55b
Finchingfield	31d	Frinton	32c
Finchley	19a	Friockheim	88a
Findhorn	94a	Frodsham	46a
Findochty	95b	Frome	16c
Findon	11d	Frosterley	60a
Finedon	30a	Fulford	55a
Finnart	79d	Fulwood	52c
Finstown	101c	Fyfield	19b
Fionnphort	77a	Fyvie	96c
Fishbourne	10c		
Fishguard	21b	**G**	
Fishnish	84c		
Fiskavaig	89d	Gaerwen	43b
Fittleworth	11b	Gailey	35b
Flamborough	56a	Gainford	60a
Flax Bourton	15d	Gainsborough	49a
Fleet	18c	Gairloch	90a
Fleetwood	51b	Gairlochy	85a
Flimby	57a	Gairlogie	96c
Flimwell	13c	Galashiels	75c
Flint	45d	Galgate	51b
Flitsham	39b	Galson	103b
Flyford Flavell	28a	Galston	72a
Folkestone	14c	Gardenstown	96a

Garforth	54c	Godstone	12a
Gargrave	53a	Goginan	33c
Garlieston	64c	Golders Green	19a
Garlogie	88b	Golspie	99d
Garmouth	94b	Goodwick	21b
Garstang	51b	Goole	55d
Garston	45b	Gordonstoun	94a
Garth (Powys)	26a	Gorebridge	74b
Garth (Mid Glam)	24c	Goring	17b
Gartmore	80c	Gorleston	42c
Gartocharn	79d	Gosfield	32c
Garvald	82d	Gosforth	68c
Garve	92a	Gosport	10c
Garynahine	103b	Goudhurst	13d
Gatehouse of Fleet	64c	Gourock	79d
Gateshead	68c	Govan	73a
Geddington	37d	Gramisdale	103c
Gedney Drove End	39a	Grampound	2a
George Nympton	6a	Grange (Cumbria)	51b
Gerrards Cross	18a	Grangemouth	81c
Giffnock	73a	Grantham	37b
Gifford	82d	Granthouse	76a
Gilfach Goch	24c	Grantown-on-Spey	94c
Gillingham (Dorset)	8b	Grasmere	57b
Gillingham (Kent)	20c	Grassington	53b
Gills	101b	Gravesend	20a
Gilwern	26d	Grayrigg	58c
Girtford	30b	Great Ayton	61d
Girvan	63b	Great Baddow	20a
Gisburn	53a	Great Bradfield	31d
Glamis	87d	Great Chart	13b
Glasgow	73a	Great Chesterford	31c
Glastonbury	8a	Great Driffield	56a
Glenbarr	70c	Great Dunmow	31d
Glenbrittle	89d	Great Harwood	52c
Glencarse	81b	Great Malvern	27b
Glencoe	85c	Great Missenden	18a
Glendevon	81b	Great Musgrave	59b
Glenelg	90c	Great Offley	30d
Glenfinnan	84b	Great Smeaton	60d
Glenluce	63d	Greatstone-on-Sea	14c
Glenrothes	82c	Great Torrington	5b
Glossop	47b	Great Weldon	37d
Gloucester	28c	Great Witley	27b
Glyn Neath	24a	Great Yarmouth	42d
Glyncorrwg	24a	Green Hammerton	54a
Glyntaw	23b	Greenfield	45a
Gnoshall	35b	Greenhead	66d
Goathland	62c	Greenlaw	75d
Godalming	11a	Greenloaning	80b
Godmanchester	30b	Greenock	79d
Godshill (Hants)	9b	Greenodd	57d
Godshill (I.of W.)	10c	Greenwich	19b

Gretna	65d	Haroldswick	104b
Gretna Green	65d	Harpenden	30d
Greystoke	58a	Harrietsham	20c
Grimsby	50a	Harrogate	54a
Gringley on the Hill	49a	Harrow	18b
Grinton	60c	Hart	61b
Grizebeck	57d	Hartfield	12a
Groby	37c	Hartland	5b
Groombridge	12a	Hartlebury	28a
Gruinard	97a	Hartlepool	60b
Gruinart	69a	Hartley Wintney	18c
Guildford	11b	Harwell	17b
Guisborough	61b	Harwich	32d
Guiseley	53d	Hascombe	11a
Gullane	82c	Haslemere	11a
Gunnislake	3b	Haslingden	52c
Guyhirn	38d	Hastings	13d
Gwbert-on-Sea	22a	Hatfield (Herts)	19a
		Hatfield (S.Yorks)	48b
H		Hatherleigh	6c
		Hathersage	47b
Haddenham	31a	Havant	10b
Haddington	75a	Haverfordwest	21d
Hadleigh (Suffolk)	32c	Haverhill	31b
Hadleigh (Essex)	20a	Hawes	59d
Hailsham	12d	Hawick	75c
Hale	46b	Hawkhurst	13d
Halesowen	28a	Hawkshead	57d
Halesworth	40d	Haworth	53d
Halford	28b	Haxey	49a
Halifax	53d	Hay-on-Wye	26d
Halkirk	100d	Haydon Bridge	67d
Halland	12c	Hayle	1d
Halloughton	48d	Haytor Vale	4a
Hallsands	4c	Haywards Heath	12a
Halstead	32c	Heacham	39b
Halton Gill	52b	Headcorn	13b
Haltwhistle	66d	Heanor	36b
Halwell	4c	Heathfield	13c
Ham Street	13d	Hebden Bridge	53d
Hamble	10a	Heckfield	18c
Hambledon	10a	Heckington	38a
Hamilton	73a	Heckmondwike	53d
Hampstead	19a	Heddon on the Wall	68c
Hampton	18d	Hedon	56c
Handsworth (Yorks)	48a	Heiton	75d
Hanley	46d	Helensburgh	79d
Harbottle	67b	Helmsdale	99b
Hardwicke	27d	Helmsley	61d
Harlech	44c	Helsby	46a
Harleston	42a	Helston	1d
Harlow	19b	Hemel Hempstead	18b
Harmerhill	34b	Hemsby	42d

Hendon	19a	Honington	32a
Henfield	11d	Honiton	7d
Henley in Arden	28b	Hook (Hants)	18c
Henley-on-Thames	18a	Hope Bowdler	34d
Henlow	30d	Hope under Dinmore	27a
Henstridge	8b	Horbury	54c
Hereford	27c	Horley	12a
Hermitage	17d	Horncastle	50c
Herne	14a	Horndean	10b
Herne Bay	14a	Hornden	20a
Hertford	19b	Horns Cross	5b
Hessle	56c	Hornsea	56a
Heswall	45b	Horsforth	54c
Hethersett	42a	Horsham	11b
Hetton le Hole	68d	Horton in Ribblesdale	52b
Hexham	67d	Horwich	46a
Heysham	51b	Houghton-le-Spring	68d
Heywood	46b	Hounslow	18d
Hibaldstow	49b	Hove	12c
High Bentham	52a	Hovingham	55a
Highclere	17c	Howden	55d
High Hampton	5d	Hownam	75d
High Hawsker	62c	Hoxne	41b
High Hesket	58a	Hoylake	45b
High Wycombe	18a	Hucknall	48c
Highworth	16b	Huddersfield	53d
Hilborough	39d	Huggate	55b
Hilderthorpe	56a	Hull	56c
Hillswick	104a	Humberstone	50a
Hinckley	36d	Huna	101b
Hinderwell	62a	Hunford	72a
Hindhead	11a	Hungerford	17c
Hindley	46a	Hunmanby	56a
Hintlesham	32b	Hunstanton	39b
Hirwaun	24a	Huntingdon	30b
Histon	31a	Huntley	95b
Hitchin	30d	Hurstbourne Tarrant	17c
Hobkirk	75d	Hurstmonceux	13c
Hockering	42b	Hurstpierpoint	12c
Hoddesdon	19a	Hurworth	61a
Hodnet	35a	Husbands Bosworth	37c
Holbeach	38b	Hutton Rudby	61d
Holkham	39b	Hyde	47a
Holme (Cumbria)	58c	Hythe (Kent)	14c
Holme (Humberside)	55d	Hythe (Hants)	10a
Holmes Chapel	46d		
Holmfirth	47b	**I**	
Holsworthy	3a		
Holt	40a	Ibsley	9b
Holyhead	43b	Ibstock	36b
Holytown	73b	Ilchester	8a
Holywell	45c	Ilfracombe	6a
Homersfield	42a	Ilkestone	36b

Ilkley	53d	Jarrow	68
Ilminster	7b	Jedburgh	75
Immingham	56c	John o' Groats	101
Inchbare	88c	Johnston	21
Inchnadamph	97d	Johnstone	72
Inchture	82a		
Indian Queens	2a	**K**	
Inellan	79d		
Ingatestone	20a	Kames	78
Ingbirchworth	47b	Kegworth	37
Ingleton	52a	Keighley	53
Ingoldmells	50d	Keills	77
Innerleithen	74d	Keiss	101
Insch	95d	Keith	95
Insh	86a	Keld	59
Inveralligin	90a	Kelham	49
Inverallochy	96b	Kellybray	2
Inveraray	78b	Kelmarsh	29
Inverbeg	79d	Kelsall	46
Inverbervie	88c	Kelso	75
Inverewe	97a	Kelty	81
Inverey	87a	Kelvedon	32
Inverfarigaig	92c	Kemnay	96
Invergarry	85b	Kempston	30
Invergordon	93b	Kendal	58
Inverinate	91c	Kenilworth	28
Inverkeilor	88c	Kenmore	86
Inverkeithing	81d	Kenn	15
Inverkip	71b	Kennacraig	70
Inverkirkaig	97b	Kenninghall	42
Invermoriston	92c	Kessingland	42
Inverness	93a	Kessock	92
Inversanda	84d	Keston	19
Invershiel	90d	Keswick	57
Invershin	99a	Kettering	30
Inversnaid	79b	Kettlebridge	82
Inverurie	96c	Kettlewell	53
Ipswich	32b	Keynsham	15
Irlam	46a	Kibworth Harcourt	37
Ironbridge	35c	Kidderminster	28
Irthlingborough	30a	Kidlington	29
Irvine	71b	Kidsgrove	47
Isbister	104a	Kidwelly	22
Isle of Whithorn	64c	Kilbarchan	72
Isleham	31b	Kilberry	70
Itchen	10a	Kilbirnie	71
Itchen Stoke	10a	Kilburn	61
Ivybridge	3d	Kilchattan	71
Ivychurch	14d	Kilchenzie	70
		Kilchoan	83
J		Kilchrenan	78
		Kilconquhar	82
Jamestown	79d	Kilcreggan	79

...onan	99d	Kippford	65c
...inan	78c	Kirby Hill	54a
...hampton	5d	Kirby Malzeard	53b
...ean	70a	Kirkaldy	82c
...mster	101b	Kirkbampton	65d
...n	80a	Kirkbean	65c
...ngworth	68c	Kirkbride	65d
...nalcom	71b	Kirkby	45b
...naluag	89b	Kirkby Lonsdale	58c
...narnock	72a	Kirkbymoorside	62c
...nartin	78c	Kirkby Stephen	59b
...naurs	72a	Kirkcolm	63a
...nelford	78a	Kirkconnel	72d
...nichael	78c	Kirk Deighton	54a
...norach	92a	Kirkfieldbank	73b
...nory	78c	Kirkham	51d
...nun	79d	Kirkliston	74a
...inver	78a	Kirkmichael	87c
...sea	56d	Kirknewton	76c
...enny	82b	Kirkoswald	71d
...by	29b	Kirkpatrick Fleming	65d
...vinning	71b	Kirkudbright	64d
...berley	42a	Kirkwall	101d
...brace	100c	Kirriemuir	87d
...cardine	81d	Kirton (Humberside)	49b
...cardine O'Neil	88a	Kirton (Lincs)	38b
...craig	86b	Knaresborough	54a
...ghorn	82c	Knarsdale	66d
...gsbarns	82b	Knighton	26b
...gsbridge	4c	Knockandhu	94c
...gsclere	17d	Knottingley	54c
...gsdown	19d	Knutsford	46b
...gsgate	14b	Kyle of Lochalsh	90c
...g's Heath	36c	Kyleakin	90c
...g's Langley	18b	Kylerhea	90c
...g's Lynn	39a	Kylestrome	98c
...gs Norton	28a		
...gs Somborne	9b	**L**	
...gsteignton	4a		
...gston Bagpuize	17a	Laceby	50a
...gston upon Thames	18d	Lacock	16c
...gswear	4c	Ladbroke	29a
...gussie	86a	Ladybank	82a
...ochbervie	98d	Lagg	77d
...ochewe	90b	Laggan Bridge	86a
...och Hourn	84b	Laide	97a
...ochleven	85c	Lairg	99a
...ochmoidart	84a	Lakenheath	39d
...och Rannoch	86c	Lamberhurst	13c
...oss	94a	Lambourn	17a
...ross	81b	Lamlash	70a
...tore	96c	Lampeter	25b
...pax	54c	Lamphey	21d

Lanark	73b	Leslie	
Lancaster	51b	Lesmahagow	
Lanchester	68c	Letchworth	
Landford	9b	Letheringsett	
Lands End	1c	Leuchars	
Lane End	18a	Leven	
Langholm	66a	Leven	
Langport	7b	Leverburgh	1
Langtoft	56a	Lewes	
Lanivet	2a	Lewisham	
Lapford	6c	Leyburn	
Larbert	81c	Leyland	
Largo	82a	Leysdown	
Largo Ward	82a	Lhanbryde	
Largs	71b	Libberton	
Larkhall	73b	Lichfield	
Larling	40c	Lifton	
Lastingham	62c	Lilliesleaf	
Latheron	101a	Limpsfield	
Lauder	75a	Lincoln	
Laugharne	22c	Lindores	
Laughton	12c	Lingdale	
Launceston	3a	Linlithgow	
Laurencekirk	88a	Linslade	
Laurieston	64c	Lintmill	
Lavenham	32a	Linton	
Lawers	86c	Linwood	
Lawton	46d	Liphook	
Laxey	51c	Liskeard	
Lazonby	58a	Liss	
Leadburn	74a	Littleborough	
Leadenham	49d	Littlebourne	
Leadgate	68c	Littlehampton	
Leadhills	73d	Little Ouseburn	
Leasingham	49d	Littleport	
Leatherhead	18d	Littlestone-on-Sea	
Lechlade	16b	Little Stukeley	
Leconfield	56c	Little Thurlow	
Ledbury	27d	Liverpool	
Lee on the Solent	10c	Liversedge	
Leeds	54c	Lizard	
Leedstown	1d	Llanaber	
Leek	47c	Llanaelhaearn	
Leeming	61c	Llanbedr	
Legbourne	50a	Llanbedrog	
Leicester	37c	Llanberis	
Leigh (Grtr Manchester)	46a	Llanbrynmair	
Leigh on Sea	20a	Llanddewi	
Leighton Buzzard	30c	Llandeilo	
Leiston	41d	Llandinam	
Lendalfoot	63b	Llandissilio	
Leominster	27a	Llandovery	
Lerwick	104b	Llandrillo	

ndrindod Wells	26a	Lochgilphead	78c
ndudno	44a	Lochgoilhead	79d
ndyssul	22b	Lochinver	97b
nelli	22d	Lochmaben	65b
nerchymedd	43b	Lochmaddy	103c
nfaethlu	43b	Lochranza	70a
nfair Caereinion	34c	Lochwinnoch	71b
nfairfechan	44a	Lockerbie	65b
nfair Talhaiarn	44b	Loddon	42c
nfihangel	26d	Loftus	62a
nfrynach	26c	Loggerheads	35b
nfyllin	34a	Logierait	86d
ngadog	23b	London	19a
ngamarch Wells	26a	London Colney	18b
ngefni	43b	Long Bennington	37b
ngelynin	33c	Longbenton	68c
ngennith	22d	Long Compton	28d
ngoed	44a	Long Crendon	17b
ngollen	34a	Long Eaton	37a
ngurig	33d	Longforgan	82a
ngwnnadl	43c	Longformacus	75b
ngybi	25b	Longframlington	68a
ngynog	34a	Longhorsley	68a
nidloes	33d	Longhoughton	68a
nmadoc	22d	Long Newton	60b
non	23a	Longniddry	82c
nrwst	44b	Long Preston	53a
nsantffraid	25a	Longridge	52c
nsawel	25d	Long Sutton (Lincs)	39a
nsoy	15a	Long Sutton (Somerset)	8a
nthony	26d	Longtown	66c
ntrisant	24c	Looe, E. & W.	3c
ntwit Major	24c	Lossiemouth	94b
nuwchllyn	33b	Lostwithiel	2b
nwrtyd Wells	26a	Loughborough	37a
nybyther	25c	Louth	50a
nymynech	34a	Lowestoft	42c
nyre	26a	Lowick	76c
chryd	22a	Ludag	103c
drod	25b	Ludgershall	17c
vyngwril	33a	Ludlow	27a
swen	26c	Lumphanan	88a
anhead	74a	Lumsden	95d
ans	71d	Luss	79d
chailort	84a	Luton	30d
chaline	84c	Lutterworth	29b
charbriggs	65a	Lybster	101c
chboisdale	103c	Lydd	14c
chbuie	77b	Lydford	3b
chcarron	90b	Lydney	15b
chearnhead	80a	Lyme Regis	7d
chgair	78c	Lyminge	14a
chgelly	81d	Lymington	9d

Lymm	46a	Markfield	3
Lympne	14c	Markinch	8
Lyndhurst	9b	Marksbury	1
Lyneham	16a	Marlborough	1
Lyness	101c	Marlow	1
Lynmouth	6a	Marple	4
Lynton	6a	Marsden (W.Yorks)	4
Lytchett Minster	9c	Marshfield	1
Lytham St.Annes	51d	Martock	
		Marton (Lincs)	4
M		Maryculter	8
		Marykirk	8
Mablethorpe	50b	Maryport	5
Macclesfield	46d	Masham	6
Macduff	95b	Matlock	4
Machen	24d	Mauchline	7
Machrihanish	69d	Maxton	7
Machynlleth	33c	Maybole	7
Mackworth	36b	Mayfield	1
Macmerry	74b	Measham	3
Maesteg	23d	Meigle	8
Maghull	45b	Meikleour	8
Magor	15a	Melbourn	3
Maiden Bradley	8b	Melbourne	3
Maidenhead	18a	Melksham	1
Maiden Newton	8c	Mellon Charles	9
Maidens	71d	Melness	10
Maidstone	13b	Melrose	7
Maldon	20a	Melsonby	6
Malham	53a	Meltham	4
Mallaig	84a	Melton Mowbray	3
Malmesbury	16a	Melvaig	9
Malpas	34b	Melvich	10
Maltby	48a	Menai Bridge	4
Malton	55b	Meopham	2
Malvern Wells	27d	Mere	
Manchester	47a	Merrivale	
Mangotsfield	15b	Merthyr Tydfil	2
Manningtree	32d	Messingham	4
Manorbier	21d	Methil	8
Mansfield	48c	Methlick	9
Marazion	1c	Methven	8
March	38d	Methwold	3
Maresfield	12a	Mettingham	4
Margam	23d	Mevagissey	
Margate	14b	Mexborough	4
Mark	15c	Mid Calder	7
Market Deeping	38a	Middleham	6
Market Drayton	35a	Middlemarsh	
Market Harborough	37d	Middlesborough	6
Market Rasen	49b	Middleton (Norfolk)	3
Market Warsop	48c	Middleton in Teesdale	5
Market Weighton	55d	Middlewich	4

lidgeholme	66d
lidhurst	11c
lid-Lavant	11c
lidsomer Norton	15d
lid Yell	104b
lildenhall	31b
lilford (Surrey)	11a
lilford Haven	21d
lillerston	72b
lillmeece	35b
lillom	57d
lillport	71b
lilnathort	81b
lilnthorpe	51b
lilovaig	89a
lilton	9d
lilton Abbot	3b
lilton Keynes	30c
lilverton	7a
linehead	6b
linster (Kent, I.of Sheppey)	20d
linster (Kent)	14a
linsterley	34d
lintlaw	96b
lirfield	53c
listerton (Notts)	49a
listerton (Somerset)	8a
litford	68a
lobberley	46b
lodbury	3d
loelfre	44a
loffat	74c
lold	45d
loniaive	64b
lonifieth	82b
lonkleigh	5b
lonks Eleigh	41a
lonkton	72c
lonmouth	27c
lontgomery	34c
lontrose	88c
lonyash	47d
lonymusk	95d
lorar	84a
lorecambe	51b
loresby	57c
loreton in Marsh	28d
loretonhampstead	4a
lorley	54c
lorpeth	68a
lorriston	23b
lortehoe	5b
lortimers Cross	27a
Mossat	94d
Motherwell	73b
Mountain Ash	24a
Mountsorrel	37a
Mousehole	1c
Mouswald	65d
Mowtie	88b
Muchalls	88b
Much Birch	27c
Much Hadham	31c
Much Wenlock	35c
Muddleswood	11d
Muir of Fowlis	95d
Muir of Ord	92a
Muirdrum	82b
Muirhead	82a
Muirkirk	73c
Muker	59d
Mullion	1d
Mumbles	23d
Mumby	50d
Mundesley	40b
Munlochy	93a
Murlaggan	84b
Musselburgh	74b
Muthill	81a
Mybster	101b

N

Nafferton	56a
Nailsea	15d
Nailsworth	16a
Nairn	93b
Nant-y-Moel	24c
Nantgarw	24c
Nantwich	46c
Narberth	22c
Narborough	37c
Neath	23d
Needham Market	32b
Neilston	72a
Nelson (Lancs)	52d
Nelson (Mid Glam)	24a
Nenthead	67d
Nenthorn	75d
Nesscliff	34b
Neston	45b
Nether Stowey	7b
Netherwitten	68a
Nethy Bridge	94c
New Abbey	65c
New Aberdour	96a

Newark-on-Trent	49c	Ninfield	13
Newbiggin-by-the-Sea	68a	Nordelph	39
Newbigging	73b	Norham	76
Newbridge	24b	Norman Cross	38
Newbridge-on-Wye	26a	Normanton	54
Newburgh	82a	Northallerton	60
Newburgh	96d	Northampton	29
Newburn	68c	North Bersted	11
Newbury	17d	North Berwick	82
Newcastle Emlyn	22a	North Cave	55
Newcastle-under-Lyme	35b	North Elmhall	40
Newcastle-upon-Tyne	68c	North Ferriby	55
Newcastleton	66a	North Frodingham	56
New Cumnock	72c	Northiam	13
New Deer	96a	Northleach	28
Newent	27d	North Petherton	7
New Galloway	64a	Northolt	18
Newhaven	12c	North Queensferry	81
New Holland	56c	North Somercotes	50
Newingreen	14c	North Sunderland	76
Newlyn	1c	North Tawton	6
Newmachar	96c	North Thoresby	50
Newmarket	31b	North Tidworth	16
New Mills	47a	North Tolsta	103
Newmilns	72a	North Walsham	40
Newnham	27d	Northwich	46
New Pitsligo	96a	Norwich	40
Newport (Salop)	35b	Nottingham	37
Newport (Dyfed)	21b	Nuneaton	36
Newport (Gwent)	15a	Nunthorpe	61
Newport (I.o.W.)	10c	Nutley	12
Newport Pagnell	30c		
Newport-on-Tay	82a	**O**	
New Quay	25a		
Newquay	2a	Oadby	37
New Romney	14c	Oakham	37
New Scone	81b	Oakhill	15
New Seaham	68d	Oakworth	53
Newton Abbot	4a	Oban	78
Newton Arlosh	65d	Occumster	101
Newton Aycliffe	60a	Ochiltree	72
Newton Ferrers	3d	Ockley	11
Newtongrange	75a	Ogmore	24
Newton-le-Willows	46a	Okehampton	3
Newton on the Moor	68a	Old Dailly	63
Newtonmore	86a	Oldham	47
Newton Poppleford	7c	Old Leake	50
Newton Stewart	64c	Oldmeldrum	96
Newtown	34c	Ollaberry	104
Newtown St. Boswells	75d	Ollerton	48
Newtyle	87d	Olney	30
Neyland	21d	Onchan	51
Nigg	93b	Ordie	87

Orford	41c	Pencaitland	75a
Ormesby St. Margaret	42d	Penderyn	24a
Ormiston	82c	Pendine	22c
Ormskirk	45b	Penegoes	33d
Orpington	19d	Penicuik	74a
Orton	59a	Penistone	47b
Ossett	54c	Penketh	46a
Ossington	48d	Penkridge	35b
Oswaldkirk	54b	Penmaenmawr	44a
Oswaldtwistle	52c	Pennal	33c
Oswestry	34b	Penrith	58a
Otford	19d	Penryn	2c
Otley	53d	Pensford	15d
Otterbourne	10a	Penshurst	12a
Otterburn	67b	Pentraeth	44a
Otter Ferry	78c	Pentrebont	25b
Otterswick	104b	Pentre-Foelas	44d
Ottery St. Mary	7c	Penzance	1c
Oundle	38c	Perranporth	1b
Outwell	39c	Pershore	28a
Overbister	101d	Perth	81b
Overstrand	40b	Peterborough	38c
Overton (Clwyd)	34b	Peterculter	88b
Overton (Hants)	17d	Peterhead	96b
Over Whiteacre	36c	Peterlee	60b
Oxford	17b	Petersfield	10b
Oykel Bridge	97d	Petworth	11a
		Pevensey	12d
P		Pewsey	16d
		Philleigh	2c
Paddock Wood	13a	Pickering	55b
Padstow	2a	Piddletrenthide	8c
Paignton	4c	Piercebridge	61a
Painswick	16a	Pierowall	101d
Paisley	72a	Pinchbeck	38a
Pangbourne	17b	Piperspool	3a
Parkeston	32d	Pirnmill	70a
Parracombe	6a	Pitlochry	86d
Paston	40b	Pitscottie	82a
Pateley Bridge	53b	Pitsea	20a
Pathhead	74b	Pittentrail	99b
Patna	72c	Pittenweem	82d
Patrington	56a	Playden	13d
Peak Forest	47b	Plean	80d
Peasemarsh	13d	Plockton	90c
Peasenhall	41d	Pluckley	13b
Peebles	74a	Plymouth	3d
Peel	51c	Plympton	3d
Pembroke	21d	Pocklington	55b
Pembroke Dock	21d	Polbathic	3c
Pembury	13a	Polegate	12d
Penally	22c	Polmont	81d
Penarth	24d	Polperro	2b

Polzeath	2a	Prestatyn	45a
Ponders End	19b	Presteigne	26b
Pontardawe	23b	Preston (Lancs)	52c
Pontardulais	23b	Preston (Dorset)	8c
Pontefract	54c	Preston Brockhurst	35a
Ponteland	68c	Preston Candover	10a
Pontrhydfendigaid	25b	Prestonpans	82c
Pontyates	23a	Prestwick	71c
Pontypool	15a	Princes Risborough	18a
Pontypridd	24c	Princetown	3b
Poole	9c	Probus	2a
Poolewe	97a	Prudhoe	68c
Porlock	6b	Puckeridge	31c
Port Appin	84d	Puddletown	8c
Port Askaig	69b	Pudsey	53c
Port Bannantyne	71b	Pulborough	11b
Port Charlotte	69a	Pulham	42a
Port Ellen	69a	Purfleet	19b
Port Erin	51c	Purton	16b
Port Glasgow	79d	Pwllheli	43d
Portgower	99d	Pycombe	12c
Porth	24c		
Porth-y-Rhydd	22d	**Q**	
Porthcawl	23d		
Porthleven	1d	Queenborough	20d
Porthmadog	33a	Queensferry	45c
Porthowen	1b	Quorn	37a
Port Isaac	2a		
Portishead	15a	**R**	
Portknockie	95b		
Portlethen	88b	Radcliffe (Grtr Manchester)	46b
Portloe	2c	Radcliffe on Trent	37a
Port Logan	63c	Radlett	19a
Portmahomack	99c	Radstock	15d
Portnacroish	84d	Raglan	15a
Portnaguiran	103b	Rainford	46a
Portnahaven	69d	Rainham	19b
Port of Menteith	80a	Rampside	51b
Port of Ness	103b	Ramsbottom	52c
Portpatrick	63c	Ramsey (Cambs)	38c
Portree	89b	Ramsey (I.o.M.)	51c
Portskerra	100c	Ramsgate	14b
Portsmouth	10d	Ranby	48b
Portsonachan	78b	Rapness	101a
Portsoy	95b	Rathen	96b
Port Talbot	23d	Ratlinghope	34d
Port William	63d	Rattray	87d
Potterne	16c	Raund	30a
Potter's Bar	19a	Ravenglass	57d
Potton	30b	Ravenscar	62d
Poulton-le-Fylde	51d	Rawcliffe	55c
Prees	35a	Rawmarsh	48a
Prescot	46a	Rawtenstall	52d

Rayleigh	20a	Romanno Bridge	74a
Reading	17d	Romford	19b
Reculver	14a	Romiley	47a
Redcar	61b	Romsey	9b
Redcastle	92a	Ropley	10a
Redditch	28a	Rosehearty	96a
Redhill	12a	Rosemarkie	92b
Redruth	1d	Roskhill	89a
Reedham	42c	Roslin	74a
Reepham	42b	Ross-on-Wye	27d
Reeth	60c	Rosyth	81d
Reigate	11b	Rothbury	67b
Reiss	101b	Rotherham	48a
Rempstone	37a	Rothesay	71b
Renfrew	72a	Rothes-on-Spey	94a
Repton	36b	Rothwell (W.Yorks)	54c
Resolven	23b	Rothwell (Northants)	37d
Revesby	50c	Rottingdean	12c
Reydon	41d	Roughton	40a
Rhayader	26a	Roxton	30b
Rhiconich	98c	Royal Leamington Spa	29a
Rhondda	24a	Royal Tunbridge Wells	12b
Rhosli	22d	Roybridge	85b
Rhosneigr	43a	Royston	31c
Rhos-on-Sea	44b	Royton	47a
Rhuddan	45a	Ruabon	45d
Rhyd-Owen	25a	Rudston	56a
Rhyl	44b	Rugby	29b
Rhymney	24a	Rugeley	36a
Rhyne	95d	Runcorn	46a
Richborough	14b	Rushden	30a
Richmond	60c	Ruskington	49d
Richmond upon Thames	18d	Rutherglen	72a
Rickmansworth	18b	Ruthin	45c
Riding Mill	67d	Ruthven	87d
Ridsdale	67b	Ryde	10c
Rievaulx	61d	Rye	13d
Ringford	64c	Ryhope	68d
Ringmer	12c	Rylstone	52b
Ringwood	9d	Ryton	68c
Ripley (Derbys)	48c		
Ripley (Surrey)	11b	S	
Ripon	54a		
Roade	29b	Sadberge	60b
Roberton	74d	Saffron Walden	31d
Robertsbridge	13c	St.Abbs	76a
Robin Hood's Bay	62d	St.Agnes	1b
Rochdale	52d	St.Albans	18b
Rochester	13a	St.Andrews	82b
Rochford	20a	St.Asaph	45c
Rock	2a	St.Austell	2a
Rodel	103b	St.Bees	57a
Rogate	11a	St.Blazey	2b

St. Buryan	1c	Saundersfoot	22c
St. Catherines	78b	Saxilby	49a
St. Clears	22c	Saxmundham	41a
St. Columb Major	2a	Scalby	62a
St. Columb Minor	2a	Scalloway	104c
St. Combs	96b	Scamblesby	50a
St. Cyrus	88c	Scampton	49b
St. Davids	21a	Scarborough	62a
St. Devereux	27c	Scarfskerry	101b
St. Fillans	80a	Scarinish	83a
St. Germans	3c	Scartho	50a
St. Helens (Merseyside)	46a	Scleddau	21b
St. Helens (I. of W.)	10c	Sconser	89c
St. Ives (Cornwall)	1d	Scotch Corner	61c
St. Ives (Huntingdon)	31a	Scotter	49b
St. John's Chapel	59b	Scourie	98c
St. Just	1c	Scousburgh	104c
St. Keverne	2c	Scrabster	101b
St. Leonards	13d	Scriven	54
St. Margarets at Cliffe	14b	Scrooby	48b
St. Margaret's Hope	101c	Scunthorpe	49b
St. Marys (Orkney)	101c	Seaford	12c
St. Mawes	2c	Seaham	68a
St. Mellons	24d	Seahouses	76a
St. Monans	82b	Seal	19c
St. Neots	30b	Seamer	62a
St. Ninians	81c	Seamill	71b
St. Petrox	21d	Seascale	57c
Salcombe	4c	Seaton	7c
Sale	46b	Sedbergh	58c
Salen (Highland)	84c	Sedgefield	61a
Salen (Mull)	84c	Sedgley	35c
Salford	46b	Sedlescombe	13d
Saline	81d	Seend	16
Salisbury	9b	Selborne	10b
Saltash	3d	Selby	54c
Saltburn	62a	Selkirk	75
Saltcoats	71b	Sellindge	14
Saltfleet	50a	Selly Oak	36
Sanaigmore	69a	Selsey	11
Sandbach	46d	Selstad	14
Sandbank	79c	Semington	16
Sandersted	19d	Sennen	1
Sandgate	14c	Settle	53
Sandhead	63b	Sevenoaks	13
Sandown	10c	Severn Stoke	28
Sandwich	14b	Shaftesbury	8
Sandwick	104c	Shalbourne	17
Sandy	30b	Shalford	11
Sannox	70b	Shanklin	10
Sanquhar	73d	Shap	59
Sarre	14a	Sharpness	15
Satley	60a	Sharwell	10

Shawbury	35a	Slapton	4c
Sheerness	20b	Sleaford	49d
Sheffield	48a	Sledmere	55b
Shefford	30d	Sleights	62c
Shepton Mallet	8a	Slough	18a
Sherborne	8a	Slyne	51b
Sherburn in Elmet	54c	Smailholm	75d
Shere	11b	Smithfield	66c
Sheringham	40a	Smithwick	36c
Sherston	16a	Smoo	98d
Shieldaig	90a	Snaith	55c
Shifnal	35d	Snodland	13a
Shildon	60a	Soham	31b
Shillingford	17b	Solihull	28b
Shilton	36d	Solva	21a
Shipley	53d	Somerton	8a
Shipston on Stour	28d	Sompting	11d
Shipton-under-Wychwood	28d	Sonning	18c
Shoeburyness	20b	Sorn	72c
Shoreham by Sea	11d	Soulby	58b
Shotley	41a	Sourton	3b
Shotley Bridge	68c	Southall	18b
Shotton	45d	Southam	29a
Shotts	73b	Southampton	9b
Shrewsbury	34b	South Brent	4c
Shrivenham	17a	Southend-on-Sea	20a
Sidcot	15c	Southery	39c
Sidcup	19d	South Ferriby	55d
Siddington	46d	South Harting	10b
Sidford	7d	South Hayling	10d
Sidlesham	10d	South Kelsey	49b
Sidmouth	7c	South Kilvington	61d
Silkstone	47b	South Mimms	19a
Silloth	65d	Southminster	20b
Silsden	53b	South Molton	6a
Silverdale	51b	South Ockendon	19b
Silverstone	29d	South Otterington	61d
Simonburn	67d	South Petherton	7b
Simonsbath	6b	Southport	51d
Singleton	11c	South Queensferry	81d
Sissinghurst	13d	Southsea	10c
Sittingbourne	13b	South Shields	68d
Sixpenny Handley	9a	Southwell	48d
Skaill	101c	Southwold	41d
Skegness	50d	Sowerby Bridge	53d
Skelmersdale	46a	Spalding	38b
Skelmorlie	71b	Sparkford	8a
Skelton	61b	Spean Bridge	85a
Skewen	23b	Spennymoor	60a
Skipsea	56a	Spetchley	28a
Skipton	52d	Spey Bay	94b
Slaidburn	52a	Spilsby	50c
Slammanan	81c	Spinningdale	99a

Spittal

Spittal	76a	Stoke-on-Trent	35b
Spittal of Glenshee	87c	Stokenchurch	18a
Spofforth	54a	Stokesay	27a
Springholm	64b	Stokesley	61c
Sproatley	56c	Stone (Staffs)	35b
Sprouston	75d	Stone (Glos)	15b
Stadhampton	17b	Stonehaven	88b
Staffin	89b	Stonehouse	16a
Stafford	35b	Stoneykirk	63c
Stagsden	30a	Stonor	18a
Staindrop	60a	Stony Stratford	29c
Staines	18d	Stornoway	103b
Staithes	62a	Storrington	11c
Stalbridge	8b	Stourbridge	28a
Stalybridge	47a	Stourport	27b
Stamford	38c	Stow (Borders)	75c
Stamford Bridge	54b	Stow on the Wold	28c
Standish	46a	Stowmarket	32a
Stanford le Hope	20c	Strachan	88a
Stanhope	59b	Stradsett	39c
Stanley (Durham)	68c	Stranraer	63c
Stanley (Tayside)	81b	Stratford St.Mary	32c
Stanlow	45b	Stratford-upon-Avon	28b
Stanmore	18b	Strathaven	72b
Stannington	68a	Strathcanaird	97c
Stanstead Abbots	19b	Strathmiglo	81b
Stansted	31d	Strathpeffer	92a
Stapleford	37a	Strathy	100c
Staplehurst	13b	Strathyre	80a
Starcross	4b	Stratton	5c
Staveley (Cumbria)	58c	Streatley	17b
Staveley (Derbys)	48c	Street	8a
Staxton	56a	Strensall	55a
Stein	89a	Stretford	46b
Stenhousemuir	80d	Strichen	96a
Stepps	73a	Stromeferry	90c
Stevenage	30d	Stromness	101c
Stevenston	71b	Stronachlachar	79b
Stewarton	72a	Stronmilchan	79b
Steyning	11d	Strontian	84c
Stibb Cross	5d	Stroud	16a
Stickney	50c	Struan	86c
Stiffkey	40a	Struy	92c
Stillington	54b	Studland	9c
Stilton	38c	Studley	28a
Stirling	80d	Sturminster Newton	8b
Stithians	1d	Sturry	14a
Stock	20a	Sturton	49c
Stockbridge	9b	Sudbury	32c
Stockport	46b	Sumburgh	104
Stocksbridge	47b	Summer Bridge	53
Stockton-on-Tees	60b	Sunderland	68c
Stoke Mandeville	18a	Surbiton	18c

Sutton	19c	Terrington St.Clement	39a
Sutton Benger	16a	Tetbury	16a
Sutton Bridge	39a	Tewkesbury	28c
Sutton Coldfield	36c	Thame	17b
Sutton in Ashfield	48c	Thamesmead	19b
Sutton on Sea	50b	Thatcham	17d
Swadlincote	36b	Thetford	32a
Swainsthorpe	42a	The Witterings	10d
Swanage	9c	Thirsk	54a
Swansea	23d	Thornaby-on-Tees	60b
Swindon	16b	Thornbury	15b
Swineshead	38a	Thorne	55c
Swinton (Grtr Manchester)	46b	Thornhill	64b
Swinton (Borders)	76a	Thornton	82c
Symington	73d	Thornton Curtis	56c
Symonds Yat	27d	Thornton Dale	62c
Syston	37a	Thorpeness	41d
		Thrapston	30a
		Thropton	67b
		Thursby	65d
T		Thurso	101a
		Ticehurst	13c
Tadcaster	54c	Tichfield	10c
Tadley	17d	Tickhill	48a
Tain	99c	Tighnabruach	78d
Talerddig	33d	Tilbury	20c
Talley	23b	Tillicoultry	81c
Talybont	33c	Timberscombe	6b
Tamworth	36c	Tintagel	5c
Tannadice	87d	Tintern	15a
Tarbert (W.Isles)	103b	Tiptree	22c
Tarbert (Strathclyde)	70a	Tipton	35d
Tarbolton	72c	Tiverton	7a
Tarporley	46c	Tobermory	83d
Tarrant Hinton	9a	Toddington	30c
Tarskavaig	84a	Todhills	87d
Tarves	96c	Todmorden	53c
Tarvin	46c	Tolleshunt D'Arcy	20b
Tattershall	50c	Tolob	104c
Taunton	7b	Tomatin	93d
Tavistock	3b	Tomintoul	94c
Taynuilt	78b	Tomnavoulin	94c
Tayport	82a	Tonbridge	13a
Tayvallich	78c	Tongland	64d
Teangue	90c	Tongue	100b
Tedburn St.Mary	4a	Tonyrefail	24c
Teignmouth	4a	Topcliffe	54a
Telford	35a	Topsham	4b
Templand	65b	Torcross	4c
Templecombe	8a	Torgyle	91d
Temple Ewell	14b	Torksey	49a
Tenbury Wells	27b	Torpoint	3d
Tenby	22c	Torquay	4c
Tenterden	13d		
Terrington	54b		

Torridon	90b	Ulceby	56c
Torryburn	81d	Ullapool	97a
Torver	57c	Ulpha	57d
Toscaig	90c	Ulverston	51b
Totland	9d	Umberleigh	6a
Totnes	4c	Upavon	16d
Totton	9b	Upminster	19b
Towcester	29b	Upper Broughton	37b
Tow Law	60a	Uppingham	37d
Tranent	74b	Upstreet	14a
Trantlebeg	100c	Upton	28c
Traquair	74d	Urchfont	16c
Trawsfynydd	33a	Urmston	46b
Tredegar	24b	Usk	15a
Tredington	28d	Uttoxeter	36a
Treen	1c	Uxbridge	18b
Trefriw	44a	Uyeasound	104b
Tregaron	25b		
Tregony	2c	**V**	
Trelech	22a		
Tremadog	44c	Vange	20a
Tresla	104a	Ventnor	10c
Tricketts Cross	9c	Verwood	9a
Trimdon	60b	Voe	104a
Tring	18a		
Trochry	86d	**W**	
Troed-y-thiw	24a		
Troon	71d	Waddington (Lancs)	52a
Trowbridge	16c	Waddington (Lincs)	49d
Trowse Newton	42a	Wadebridge	2a
Trumpington	31a	Wadhurst	13c
Truro	2a	Wainfleet	50d
Tufton	21b	Wakefield	54c
Tullibody	80d	Wakes Colne	32c
Tumble	22d	Walberswick	41a
Turnberry	71d	Walkerburn	74d
Turrif	96a	Wallasey	45b
Tutbury	36a	Wallingford	17b
Tuxford	48d	Walls	104a
Twickenham	18d	Wallsend	68d
Twycross	36d	Walmer	14b
Twyford (Berks)	18a	Walpole	41d
Twyford (Hants)	10a	Walsall	36c
Twyn-Llanan	23b	Walsingham	40a
Twynholm	64c	Waltham	50a
Tydd St.Mary	38b	Waltham Abbey	19b
Tywyn	33c	Waltham Cross	19a
		Walton-on-the-Naze	32d
U		Wantage	17a
		Warboys	38d
Uckfield	12a	Warcop	59b
Ufford	41b	Wardington	29a
Uig	89b	Ware	31c

Wareham	9c	Westgate on Sea	14b
Wargrave	18a	Westhoughton	46a
Warley	36c	West Kilbride	71b
Warlingham	19c	West Lavington	16c
Warmington	29a	West Linton	74a
Warminster	16c	West Lulworth	8c
Warning	13c	West Malling	20c
Warrington	46a	West Meon	10a
Warslow	47d	West Mersea	32c
Warter	55b	Westmeston	12c
Warton	51d	West Moors	9c
Warwick	28b	Weston (Staffs)	35b
Washford	7a	Weston on the Green	29d
Washington	68c	Weston-super-Mare	15c
Watchet	7a	West Runton	40a
Waterlooville	10a	West Witton	60c
Watford	18b	Wetheral	66c
Wath Brow	57a	Wetherby	54a
Wath-upon-Dearne	48a	Weybourne	40a
Watlington	17b	Weybridge	18d
Watten	101b	Weymouth	8c
Watton	39d	Whaleybridge	47a
Watton	42a	Whalley	52c
Wear Head	59b	Wharram-le-Street	55b
Weaverham	46c	Whickham	68c
Weaverthorpe	55b	Whiddon Down	6c
Wedmore	15c	Whiltingham	76c
Weedon Bec	29b	Whipsnade	30c
Weeford	36c	Whitbeck	57d
Weem	86d	Whitburn	68d
Weeting	39d	Whitby	62a
Wellingborough	30a	Whitchurch (Hants)	17d
Wellington (Somerset)	7a	Whitchurch (Salop)	35a
Wellington (Salop)	35a	Whitehall	101d
Wells (Somerset)	15d	Whitehaven	57a
Wells (Norfolk)	39b	Whitehills	95b
Welshampton	34b	Whithorn	64c
Welshpool	34a	Whiting Bay	70d
Welwyn Garden City	19a	Whitland	22c
Wem	35a	Whitley Bay	68d
Wemyss Bay	71b	Whitney	17a
Wendens Ambo	31d	Whitstable	14a
Wendlebury	29d	Whitstone	5d
Wendover	18a	Whittington	58c
Wentbridge	54c	Whittlesey	38d
West Auckland	61a	Whitton Gilbert	68c
West Bridgford	37a	Whittonstall	58c
West Bromwich	36c	Wibsey	53d
West Burton	59d	Wick	101a
Westbury	16c	Wickford	20a
West Calder	73b	Wickham	10a
West Coker	8a	Wickham Market	41b
Westerham	19d	Wickwar	15b

Widecombe	**4a**
Widnes	**46a**
Wigan	**46a**
Wigston	**37c**
Wigton	**65d**
Wigtown	**64c**
Wilby	**41b**
Willingdon	**12d**
Willingham	**31a**
Willington	**60a**
Williton	**7a**
Wilmslow	**46b**
Wilsontown	**73b**
Wilton	**9a**
Wimborne Minster	**9c**
Wincanton	**8a**
Winchcombe	**28c**
Winchelsea	**13d**
Winchester	**10a**
Windermere	**58c**
Windsor	**18c**
Wingham	**14a**
Winkfield	**18c**
Winkleigh	**6c**
Winsford	**46c**
Winslow	**29d**
Winster	**57c**
Winterbourne (Avon)	**15b**
Winterbourne Abbas	**8c**
Winterbourne Stoke	**9a**
Winteringham	**55d**
Wirksworth	**47d**
Wisbech	**38d**
Wisborough Green	**11b**
Wishaw	**73b**
Witham	**32c**
Witheridge	**6d**
Withernsea	**56d**
Withington	**46b**
Withleigh	**6d**
Wittersham	**13d**
Witton-le-Wear	**60a**
Wiveliscombe	**7a**
Wivenhoe	**32c**
Woking	**18d**
Wokingham	**18c**
Wollaston	**30a**
Wolsingham	**60a**
Wolverhampton	**35d**
Wolverton	**17d**
Wombwell	**48a**

Woodbridge	**41a**
Woodchurch	**13d**
Woodford	**19b**
Woodhall Spa	**50c**
Woodstock	**29c**
Woodyates	**9a**
Woofferton	**27a**
Wool	**8d**
Woolacombe	**5b**
Wooler	**76c**
Woolwich	**19b**
Wooton Basset	**16b**
Worbrough	**48a**
Worcester	**28a**
Workington	**57a**
Worksop	**48a**
Worle	**15c**
Wormit	**82a**
Worthen	**34d**
Worthing	**11d**
Wotton under Edge	**16a**
Wragby	**49b**
Wrangle	**50c**
Wrexham	**45d**
Writtle	**20a**
Wrotham Heath	**20c**
Wroxham	**42b**
Wybunbury	**46c**
Wych Cross	**12a**
Wylye	**9a**
Wymondham	**42a**

Y

Yarcombe	**7b**
Yardley Gobion	**29d**
Yarm	**60b**
Yarmouth	**9d**
Yatton	**15c**
Yaxley	**38c**
Yeadon	**53d**
Yealmpton	**3d**
Yelverton	**3b**
Yeovil	**8a**
Yetholm	**76c**
Yetts of Muckart	**81d**
York	**54b**
Youlgreave	**47d**
Ysbyty Ystwyth	**25b**
Ystalyfera	**23b**
Ystradgynlais	**23b**